THE ART OF SUFFERING

THE ART OF SUFFERING

BY
LOUIS BERTRAND

TRANSLATED BY
E. F. PEELER

WITH INTRODUCTION BY
C. C. MARTINDALE, S.J.

"He who is ready to die is invincible."

CHATEAUBRIAND
Mémoires d'Outre-Tombe, Vol. III.

NEW YORK
SHEED & WARD INC.
MCMXXXVI

A TRANSLATION OF
LE LIVRE DE CONSOLATION
(COPYRIGHT : ARTHENE FAYARD ET CIE)

PRINTED IN GREAT BRITAIN

ZA 8.44.9
B46RE

41892

INTRODUCTION

WE agree that this book may require an introduction for English readers. At first, the book seems about to be devotional; then, maybe, almost cynical, and drawing by preference upon classical pagan sources to which (maybe regrettably) the bulk of our contemporary fellow-countrymen are quite unaccustomed; then, wantonly plain-spoken; and finally, to contain certain paragraphs about the Christian faith such as an unbeliever who was envious of that faith, or at least admired some of its consequences, might have written, without himself experiencing any of the certainty, joy and strength which the Catholic doctrine of suffering and death should inspire.

We realize, however, that the book is written perhaps primarily for the ordinary man (especially of the Latin stock) who has but the vaguest faith, if any. A writer, to convince such an one, has to prove that he himself is aware of all that is in his reader's mind, and this involves working his way through a mass of sentiments, ideas, allusions, even eccentricities, which the simple Catholic would wholly disregard. Our average English Catholics, even when depressed and needing consolation, would remain perfectly uninterested by what Cicero said to Cato, or by learning that Seneca's suicide was a relatively comfortable one.

However, this book, or *a* book dealing with Pain and even Death, seems to me most desirable in our times, for two opposite sorts of reasons.

The first sort of reason is the fact that very many are so unhappy, so anxious, so shaken by events that they remember (like the war), or that they are involved in (like the conditions of our 'distressed areas' or slums), or fancy they foresee (like far worse wars, or the progressive elimination of Christianity from public life), that they absolutely must be comforted and consoled. By 'consoled', I mean made to feel that they have someone who can mitigate their loneliness; an understanding friend beside them in what else were solitude: and by 'comforted', I mean strengthened, and not just cosseted.

The other sort of reason is, that men—perhaps in England especially because of its mental distance and even physical separation from the Continent—are only too ready to shove ostrich-heads into the sand, and refuse to take any cognizance of the ghastly facts of which contemporary life is full. M. Bertrand warns us that he proposes to speak with brutal frankness; there will certainly be those who will say that even so he ought not to describe human suffering so sickeningly as here and there he does. But if we never see it, and no one tells us of it, we are all too ready to believe it does not exist, and even to deny its existence. Well, for my part, I have had to nurse a man who had been as badly mutilated in body as any of those medievals that M. Bertrand describes, and far worse martyred in mind. He had escaped from Siberian prisons. I will freely say that I have had no experience comparable with that one, for strain alike nervous and spiritual. Ferocity, cruelty, all but maniac cruelty, lie but the thickness of a sheet of tissue paper beneath our 'civilization'. Unless we are somehow made aware of such things, we shall never attach a real meaning to phrases such as St. Paul uses about the terrific conflict, ever being waged, between Christ's and those who 'wander through the world for the ruin of souls' and even for the havocking of men's bodies.

Perhaps the first part, upon Old Age, is the least appealing, because (for one thing) either you are old or you are not. The serene aged men here quoted (edifying or not) are apt to say that they are glad they are no more young; but no young man would believe them. Young men will say that they don't want to be old—at least, not so old as that—and, never having experienced a lifetime's disillusionments, cannot make head or tail of what the aged are talking about, still less take their advice. Nor does the author speak, I fancy, of a life that has been so full that time races by unattended to, so that a man's age seems to him to be very much the same always, whatever his years be. And again, there is the disconcerting fact that you often perceive that at fifty you are too terribly the same person as you were at five, with the same queer prejudices, preferences, and even tricks of behaviour.

We would have liked, in this book, rather more insistence on the eternal Youth of God's Holy Spirit: "there lives the dearest freshness deep down things." The Lord is the life-giver; the soul's youth is continuously renewed—nay, invigorated, so that although, as St. Paul says, "my outer man is being worn away," an inner self is always being formed unto the stature of the maturity of Christ. He does indeed point out that *mental states*, activities of the spirit, are far better for the resisting and surmounting of pain, than any amount of momentary anæsthetics: but what the Christian wants to realize ever more and more is, that the innermost 'activity' is essentially that of Christ Himself, towards whom the "whole creation groans and travails throughout itself," so that if there *be* pain, it can become that of a spiritual Christ-birth; you may even say, the growing-pains of Christ-in-me.

In the second part, which deals directly with suffering as such (bodily, and also mental—so subtly that M. Bertrand concentrates on the suffering peculiar to 'misfits', as we say; people who, they can't see quite why, are none the less out of harmony with all of their inevitable surroundings) is a great deal of matter that is directly interesting as such; for example, the *changes* (satisfactory or not) in human sensitiveness that doctors can generalize about. Incidentally, the pages about hospitals are very striking—the change of ideal between the days when the Salpêtrière was founded that Christ might be served in the suffering Christian, and those (our own) when hospitals are but benevolent laboratories, utilitarian at all points. It is bad psychology not to notice this. A sailor recently wrote to a well-known worker in the Sea-Apostolate that such and such a Seamen's Institute was magnificent in all material ways, but had nothing, nothing, nothing in it that catered for "what we all of us have in us, though our lives are sunk in filth from the days when we crawl on to a ship as a baby-seaman till the days when we must pack up the Sea once and for all." His estimate of the seaman's life was pessimist; but not that of the Institute in question.

Now it is precisely here that the mind is so important. We keep hearing: "Why should I *suffer?*" and "Why should *I* suffer—I, manifestly innocent?" The latter is Job's question, and he had no answer save that he was unable, he so small, to read the infinite mind of God whom he knew to be righteous. Neither can the Christian adequately answer the question; but he can, once and for ever, cease to suggest that because he is innocent, he should not suffer. Who so innocent as Christ? And who, like him, so sweated blood in an Agony? As for "Why should I *suffer?*"—well, I hold that no question relating to pain can even begin to be answered if you leave out sin, which has racked the world into dislocation. Nor again if you leave out man's social solidarity. Rationalists used to say that it was unfair for God to say that the sins of the fathers should be 'visited upon' the second and the third generation. But now everyone at least perceives that a wrong can never stop still where it is. It cannot be isolated, sterilized, annihilated. It echoes and re-echoes; it spreads in concentric circles. The merest word, spoken by any man, sooner or later alters the whole interaction of the universe. I simply *am* what I am, because the whole of my ancestry was what it was;

and on what I am depends the whole of the future of the whole of the world. Naturally, the same holds true of good; and in a thousand ways I can transcend my own and even other men's bad actions, though I can never make them not to have been. But unless we introduce the redemptive suffering of Christ, we shall be forced to say that there is a lot more evil in the world than good, and that the correctives will be swamped by the *corrigenda*.

The Christian, then, being able to unite his sufferings to Christ's, need have no anxiety. As Mrs. Meynell, so acutely sensitive to suffering in any form, yet wrote: "It is not the sufferings of the innocent and holy that distress me—they know what to do with them—but those of the sinner, who wastes all of his privileges."

There is a valuable paragraph on morphia. My own experience is, first, that when pain is not intolerable, it often liberates the soul from many a distress. It may be bad enough to make you say: "I cannot do any work"; but along with that comes the infinite relief of knowing that "I did not engineer this pain—so God does not *mean* me to do any work. Or rather, the work God wants of me just now is pain; therefore my pain is workful, creative."

But then doctors may give you morphia without so much as asking your permission, when they see that the *consciousness* of pain is too weakening—pain is always weakening—that is, the cause of it is—even if you are unconscious of it: but consciousness of pain may kill you on its own, so to say. But morphia may so dull the pain as to leave your mind exceptionally free; thus during a longish period during which I was being given morphia though I didn't know it, I was able to pray with many fewer distractions and for much longer at a time than when I was having neither pain nor morphia.

But the upshot of that is: what are we to think of those, that is the Saints, who have all of the pain and none of the morphia? What must be *their* sublimity, *their* triumphant tenacity, of mind? Such that only Christ can put it into them.

Next, M. Bertrand passes to physical death. Aristotle said: "Death is of all things the most terrible, because it puts a *stop*." He said that, because he wasn't dying, and wanted above all things to *go on*. But M. Bertrand indicates, what I have seemed to notice, that most people really or supposedly dying do not find death terrible at all, nor *want* to go on. You are too cold, too tired, even too bored, to feel that anything matters much. What survives is your habitual trend of mind: if you have usually prayed, you will pray—after a fashion; but most certainly with no *intensified* faith, contrition or hope. If you are in the queer position of thinking you most certainly are dying but are none the less able to *do* something, you may think: "I had better die doing something tolerably decent"; you call on God, as you would normally do when tackling any ordinary job, but with no greater intensity than then, and would toddle forth to do something maybe quite useless and even idiotic, but which appeared to you just then as obviously requiring to be done. What you might be apprehensive of, would be the jump into something quite new. It is not true that everyone is born into the world a little Liberal *or* Conservative. Everyone is a Conservative! I will wager that even the experimentalist, the pioneer, the adventurer, has a certain dislike for the *totally* different. One's qualms may be due to one's realizing that one is about to encounter a state of being when "*I* shall be quite different." Everyone, even the maddest Cloud-Cuckoo-Land-ist, wants to remain his 'I'.

But may not one of the great 'difficulties' of dying be this—not that you have worshipped idols—loved created things too much—but that you have not loved them nearly enough? What suddenly appals one is, that God has surrounded one with a myriad things of unbelievable beauty—like butterflies, or the sea, or uneducated people—and that one has allowed them to slip by almost unnoticed. "O God, in your self-revelation, unnoticed! Oh, even when I thought I acknowledged you and worshipped you in these things of yours—that I should have done it so tamely, so poverty-strickenly! O my shame, that I should have caught and done homage to so little of you in colour, music, shape, words, contact, minds, circumambient embracing Goodness! O God, how shocked I am at myself! O my imperviousness! my letting it all slide by—not in the least because I was 'detached', wisely 'indifferent', but because of my obtuseness, my vulgarity, my spiritual anæsthesia! Of course I made some kind of response to your manifold self-offering, self-revelation; but how shamefully little I perceived of it; how seldom did I guess *you* within, creative of, all these lovely and lovable things of yours!" Well, we may make up hereafter.

Bourget wrote a book called *Le Sens de la Mort.* Not merely: "The Sense, *i.e.*, the Meaning, of Death," but "The Direction of Death," the 'whither' bodily death tends. Not indeed a mere escape from prison, an unshackling of the soul from a tomb: the body is no tomb. But the butterfly out from the chrysalis at last. My soul able to, ready to, appreciate all those things, and progressively doing so, in fact.

But again and again the Christian has to recall that it is, for him, waste of time to go on the hunt for metaphors. Never will he find anything to compare with the fact of Christ, and of the soul's union with him by grace. Certainly, these facts will not explain the whole mystery of pain and death, but they enable the Christian to make use of them and to be 'over-brimming' with joy and peace, as St. Paul so often says.

If my reason can show me that the soul is indestructible (does M. Bertrand think it can't?), and if it can surmise that in some way the soul might be reunited with a body so as to be truly human, which in its discarnate state it can hardly be said to be, my faith teaches me of my incorporation into the living Christ, so that what else can I be, save immortal, being in him? That which is "his in Christ with God" is my *life*. What the crucifixion led up to, was Resurrection. *Dux Vitae, mortuus, regnat vivus.* Even as the Father is alive, and "has life in himself," so to the Son too has he communicated that same life, and the Son has life in *himself.* And to us, co-corporate with him, he transmits that life so far as we can receive it, and it is in him that we are and must be *alive.* We *are* so; it is not merely an affair of 'shall be'. "We are called 'sons of God', and so indeed we are," says St. John. If this be so, then just in proportion as we love him in whom we are, we shall be glad to be like him in his sufferings and even in his death, and, what is even more, we shall know that we along with him are co-redemptive, and our pains and death can truly be offered with his, in an eternal Mass, for the salvation of the world.

C. C. MARTINDALE.

PREFACE

I KNOW of only one real book of consolation: *The Imitation of Christ*. The *Imitation* soars above nations and periods; its character is universal and, if one may say so, eternal. Composed for men of all times, it has no special message for the people of today. Whereas the book that lies before you now—not that it would dare to compare itself, however remotely, with any such model as the *Imitation*—is definitely influenced by anxieties peculiar to the present age.

These anxieties have given it a sombre hue, perhaps, but one cannot insist too strongly on perils which are only too real and which our habitual light-heartedness is only too willing to ignore.

It may be objected, also, that the consolations offered in this work are rather too strong meat for gentle souls; but the sole object of writing it was to rouse them out of their passivity. I should be ashamed to mislead my readers by a spurious optimism or by the offer of remedies which no serious intelligence could possibly accept. In view of the dangers that threaten the world today, and still more in view of the painful drama of every human destiny, facts must be faced with inexorable lucidity of mind and a fearless heart.

L. B.

Paris, 1933.

CONTENTS

CONTENTS

PART III

DYING

PROLOGUE

LAST June, to my great surprise, I had the pleasure of meeting my friend Jean Perbal [1] in Paris, in circumstances which were as strange as they were unforeseen.

I say "to my great surprise" because our meetings have become infrequent and very difficult, owing to the distance that separates us, and to Perbal's highly abnormal way of living. For many years he has been engaged in an important enterprise in one of the most inaccessible and least known regions of Western Africa. Formerly he used to return to France for a few months at fairly frequent intervals, to refresh his knowledge of his native land and to preserve his health, however little it may have been affected by the foreign climate. Then his visits became more rare, and finally they ceased entirely, either because his business kept him back in Africa or because the continual travelling fatigued him. Our correspondence also ceased.

I regretted it keenly, for I am lost without Perbal. He is in fact part of myself. He does my practical reasoning for me; he encourages and supports me at times of stress. And when I had that unexpected meeting with him I was suffering from a severe attack of pessimism. Not only did there seem to be no future for my country, but I was

---

[1] See my novel *Une Destinée* (published by Arthème Fayard).

continually repeating to myself that famous phrase of Grimm's: "Humanity is in desperate case." Not only did a whole world seem to be approaching its death-throes—with everything that we love and honour about to be engulfed in some undefined catastrophe—but I was in despair about myself. At the thought of decrepitude and death I felt that a host of unknown but terrifying forces were threatening the very essence of my being. I entered a realm of horrors that alternately paralysed all my energy and drove me to outbursts of panic-stricken folly. At such moments I thought of Perbal, my contemporary, who was quite likely to be experiencing the same anguish as my own. Again and again in my mind I turned to him for help. I would have written to him, although we had ceased to correspond for years, but I knew that he was a busy man burdened with heavy responsibilities and that a correspondence of this nature would have been an irksome duty for him.

I was undecided whether or not to communicate my troubles to him, when one morning in June, to my amazement, I received a note from him. In it he informed me that he was back again in Paris, staying at a hotel that was totally unknown to me, on the Butte de Montmartre, near the Sacré-Cœur, and he invited me to dine with him that evening. The note was written in the telegraphic style that he had adopted on entering on a business career and it contained not the slightest explanation of his sudden reappearance.

So Perbal was in Paris at the very moment when I needed his support. It was an instance of telepathy which impressed me without causing me undue astonishment. Each of us, no doubt, was in need of the other's assistance; each of us wanted to put his thoughts in order. But what interested me far more was why Perbal, the *habitué* of all the Grand Babylon Hotels in Europe, should want to put up at this obscure eyrie in Montmartre, close to the Basilica. It was pure caprice—of that I felt quite certain; for I was well acquainted with my old friend's whims and the curious twists and turns in his character. And then, on reflection, it occurred to me that I myself might have something to do with his choosing that outlandish spot. I had often extolled the beauty of the site and expressed my admiration for the building that had restored to a city degraded by modern industry some of its nobility of outline, a building that is unquestionably the finest example of French architecture of the nineteenth century. Moreover, I had told him about the fascination that the mere idea of the Sacred Heart has had for me ever since I was a child ; how the sound of these two words stirs the depths of my soul to tenderness as though it were a love charm. . . . I had told him about the flood of sweetness and adoration into which I seem to melt when I hear at Sunday vespers the singing of that plaintive invocation: " *Cor Jesu sacratissimum, miserere nobis!*" . . . And this wonderful symbol of human and divine fraternity, this brazier of love, had been raised like a beacon above

B 2

a city teeming with malevolence and degradation. . . .

I was not mistaken. On meeting me that evening
Perbal said to me: "It's you that made me come
here. The praises you sang of the place put the
idea into my head. I thought it would give you
pleasure, my coming to this hotel, only a stone's
throw from the Sacré-Cœur, apart from the fact
that it's a splendid hiding-place. Do you know
that this is the first time that I have been to the
Butte for thirty years? I still associated it with the
sneers of the anticlerical Press, at the time when the
Siècle was dying a natural death. . . . And now
there's hardly anyone that has ever even heard of
the *Siècle!* . . . But it wasn't only M. Homais and
his friends who vilified the Sacré-Cœur. Even the
Conservatives did—in their anxiety to be broad-
minded. Do you remember the old Marquis de
Latour-Carol who tried to stir up our enthusiasm
for the *Patrie Française*? To prove that he had no
reactionary prejudices, he poked fun at the unæs-
thetic silhouette of the Sacré-Cœur, comparing its
domes to night-caps. . . . 'You must admit, my dear
Sirs, it's simply hideous!' . . . And the same people
could find excuses for the Eiffel Tower! . . . Well,
I wanted to see if the Marquis was still right. I
did what foreigners and provincials do—came
up to Montmartre. . . . And now I am of your
opinion, only more so."

We had our dinner served in Perbal's room,
whence we could look down on the lighted city.
It was wonderful, as we sat there that evening in

4

June, to watch the unfurling of night's vast pall and its struggle with man-made illumination. My friend suddenly said to me, half in earnest, half in fun:

"Are you capable of performing an heroic deed? . . . I am sure that you have never watched the sun rise over Paris. . . . You can have a room here; we can be up in time for the first Mass; and I can promise you an infinitely better sight than this. . . ."

Early rising *is* an heroic deed for me. For years I had had to put up with it at school; it had been a daily torture. But the thought that here was an opportunity of realizing a desire that I had long been nursing, and still more the joy of sharing the feelings of my friend, decided me. I slept badly at our trysting-place. For one thing, it lay in the heart of a populous, noisy quarter; furthermore, in bidding me good-night, Perbal had said to me :

"I'm worried! Things are going badly over there. . . . I'll tell you what I mean tomorrow!"

For Perbal, who had always been so courageous and so reticent, to acknowledge his fears to me, must mean that he took a serious view of things. And this increased my own disquietude.

* * *

Next morning we were up at five o'clock. As we issued forth into the open, dawn was spreading over the city. The air was cold, and we shivered beneath our summer overcoats. On the east the grey sky

5

was slightly tinged with yellow. The whole horizon was hidden by a thick mist, whereas a light haze, as diaphanous as muslin, gradually disclosed the foreground. It was impossible as yet to distinguish Notre-Dame or the dome of the Panthéon. Only the monumental halls of the Gare du Nord and Gare de l'Est emerged. A little further off, the Buttes-Chaumont and the heights of Belleville advanced through the rain-filled clouds. . . . In the colourless dawn the whole outlook seemed to be flat and lacking in depth, and everything appeared to be so near that we were surprised to find our mighty Paris so puny. On the other side, towards the west, still thicker mists seemed to be covering the accumulations of darkness. The hills of Sèvres and Saint-Cloud were as yet invisible. To the right, we looked in vain for the dome of the Invalides and the twin towers of the Trocadéro—ghosts, whose presence was only to be sensed. But piercing the masses of steam and smoke which hung above the roof-tops—the deadly sins of a soulless generation—there rose triumphantly the colossal ugliness of the Eiffel Tower. This monstrosity, half-submerged in the mist, was the only object to be seen. I was expecting an effect of boundless space, but that was not to be. It was dull, dingy, and depressing. . . .

"I'm sorry to have disappointed you," said Perbal. "The sun won't play this morning. I'm afraid we shall have to give it up. The show's off for to-day."

As he spoke, the tolling of a bell made us turn our heads in the direction of the lofty square campanile, whose openwork silhouette dominates the whole Parisian picture. The nocturnal adoration was at an end. The first Mass would soon begin.

We entered the church, which was still in darkness, save for the feeble glimmer of a few ever-burning lamps that flickered like lost stars. On the right, a ruddy blaze near the statue of the Sacred Heart broke into the stagnant blackness beneath the vaulting. The crushing vastness of the building as seen from the narthex increased the oppressive effect of the gloom and gave me the impression of entering some sacred cavern. At first I could see nothing but the four massive piers that sustained the mighty dome, the image of heaven, the centre, the soul, of the basilica, on which converges the whole symbolism of the temple. My eyes searched the twilight of the choir for the great golden monstrance wherein the Sacrament is perpetually exposed; but all the splendours of the sanctuary seemed to slumber, as if waiting for the coming of the sun. . . .

I drew Perbal over to the life-size silver statue which represents the Sacred Heart and is surrounded by a diurnal and nocturnal Candlemas.

This statue, perhaps the most loved, the most venerated, in all the world, emerges from a thicket of burning tapers which consume themselves in flames unsparingly, glimmers in unceasing travail, little vigilant souls which palpitate, abase themselves, plunge forward in a frantic, indefatigable supplication. Before this fire all aglow with spiritual fervour we stopped an instant for a rapid prayer: a remembrance for the dead, a thought for the living. Once again I noted the tragic expression of the Christ, as though he were offering himself in vain. And the sinister phrase of the philosopher, recurring to my mind, echoed my unspoken words: "Humanity is in desperate case." Then the wavering lights, the shifting reflections, gradually changed the harrowing expression of the divine countenance, and an infinite sweetness fell from his lips. And yet the first impression persisted. As I came away I felt I was being haunted by that look, heavy with sadness and reproach—that look which seemed to say: "What have I done to you that you should abandon me like this?"

The celebrant was leaving the sacristy; Mass was about to begin in the almost empty church.

Returning to the narthex, we settled ourselves there, but no sooner had we done so than we heard the sound of voices coming from the direction of the porch, then the clumping of hob-nails, the shuffling of dilapidated footwear. We turned our heads in surprise: one would have thought the sanctuary was being invaded by a mob. We saw a batch of down-and-outs, headed by a verger, moving towards the choir—most of them timid and hesitant, stumbling against the rows of chairs, some sniggering and insolent. Perbal and I stared at each other in surprise. "What was the meaning of this curious procession?" A priest in a surplice was passing on his way to one of the confessionals, and in response to our inquiry told us: "It's the Mass for vagabonds and beggars."

8

He explained further that this, the first Mass, was said for their intentions.[1] As the poor hold the first place in the kingdom of Christ, it is only just that they should be the first to be served. Nothing is asked of them, neither prayers nor any display of piety whatsoever. They are simply invited to come in, to take part in the mystic banquet which is offered up every minute of the day and night for the whole of the human race. And when it is over—the Mass is a very short one—they are offered another kind of banquet. They are taken to the pilgrims' shelter and given a substantial meal, before they go out—their eyes still dazzled with the glittering windows and mosaics—to their life of misery and gloom. . . .

I scanned their faces as they passed. There were not so many of them as I thought—about fifty, I suppose. Most of them were men, but there were also some women with children. I recognized a trio—a man, a woman, and a child of seven or eight—whose faces were familiar to me and whose strange behaviour had for some time past attracted my attention. For weeks they had eaten their scraps of food on a seat in the Avenue Rapp, outside my house. When they had finished eating, the man and woman would wrangle and bully each other for hours on end, too drunk to move from where they were. The

[1] This Beggars' Mass is not mere fiction on my part. It actually takes place every Sunday, is extremely well attended, and presents, so I am told, a perfectly peaceful and edifying sight. The beggars of my acquaintance, whom I have here delineated, would fit with difficulty into such a setting. My sole object was to contrast their vileness with the sublime idea behind this Mass.

seat was their fief; it was one of their numerous domiciles. Then one day they would decamp, and I would see nothing more of them for several weeks. They would reappear as suddenly as they had left, the man with a heavy sack on his back, the woman dragging by the hand a little boy. It was not always the same boy. . . . Heaven knows where they picked them up. Both of the adults seemed too old to have more children of that age. Where did they come from? What was their history? They must have been foreigners—Czechs, or Rumanians, or Polish Jews. I had never actually seen them begging. They used to come with their sack stuffed with clothes and food. Sometimes they were fitted out with decent clothes, which, on their backs, soon turned into filthy rags. These people, who obstinately refused to be taken care of in a public institution, must have been maintained by some benevolent fund or charitable organization. Whenever they chanced to be in possession of a sou or two the man and woman drifted into the nearest dramshop and came back, completely drunk, to sleep on their seat in the Avenue Rapp. The child would be nearly as drunk as they, and cursing them in some outlandish tongue would tug at their grimy rags to make them leave the seat. This besotted trio—man, woman, and child—was like an abominable parody of the Holy Family. . . .

Without very much surprise I watched these denizens of the gutter pass me by. Behind them, walking with jerky steps, came a fearful-looking creature, as thin as a skeleton, reeking of alcohol, and darting fiery glances of rage and hatred in all directions. She too was dragging brutally by the hand a little child of six or seven, with a pale little face, a spiteful mouth, and wicked eyes. As I averted my gaze from these appalling faces I heard the woman saying to her neighbour in a coarse voice charged with fury:

"I? . . . I care for the priests? . . . To hell with priests! I've come here to fill my belly!"

These then were "Christ's poor" whom the verger was showing into the first row of *prie-dieux*, immediately behind the Communion rail! It was to mitigate their horrible experience of waking in the gutter that the Basilica was thrown open at break of day, that it displayed its sumptuous works in glass, its gaily gleaming enamels and mosaics. It was for their sakes that a priest was there before the altar in lace alb and golden chasuble—that God was about to offer himself in sacrifice! They were about to assist at this unheard-of thing, performed especially for them. . . . They were to take the first seats there, as the nearest relatives of the Master of the House. . . .

Meanwhile, Mass was proceeding. The warning bell rang for the Elevation, and Perbal and I were noticing the unusual emptiness of the building, when the rustle of silken garments made us turn our heads. A young woman in a cloak of white velvet trimmed with swansdown came gliding through the shadows. She was attended by two young men in evening dress: their white ties showed between the turned-up collars of their overcoats. They knelt

down a few paces away from us, behind the row of
beggars. I had a side-view of the girl: she was
adorably beautiful with her golden hair showing
through a veil of spangled gauze and her immacu-
late cloak half thrown back to reveal a magnificent
evening gown. . . . Where did they come from? . . .
What were they? Spaniards? Argentines? . . .
Were they true pilgrims or was it merely curiosity
that had brought them there? Were they revellers
from some night resort who had come for a breath
of Mass before sleeping off their nocturnal dissipation? . . . But no! These were no revellers or sight-
seers! All three, the girl especially, seemed to be
praying with such fervour, with such intensity,
that I knew not what to think. What pardon had
they come to seek? What extraordinary vow were
they fulfilling? At certain moments, when she was
absorbed in prayer, the young girl's face shone like
an angel's.

Immediately after the Elevation I said to Perbal:
"Let's go!"

I wanted to dwell on that heavenly vision. I had
no desire to see for a second time the foul-mouthed
fury or the cynical, depressing procession of the
vagabonds.

When we left the church it was fully daylight.
Once again we went towards the balustrade
encircling the platform. Almost the whole of Paris
lay open to our gaze, though objects in the distance
were still obscured by mist. By the light of the sun,
the heat from which was perceptible already, the
dullness of the buildings, the besmirchings and

befoulings of smoke and soot stood painfully self-condemned. The scene was still devoid of depth, radiance, and, above all, joy. Perbal said to me:

"I promised you a lovely sight. You must admit that what we have seen in church was far better than any sunrise, however gorgeous. . . ."

* * *

It was too early to go back to the hotel and order breakfast there.

Perbal and I have always sought out the haunts of the common people, not only for the sake of their picturesqueness but because they have a tonic effect on brain-workers. We went down the Rue Saint-Eleuthère to the little provincial Place du Tertre, where we entered a wineshop which had only just opened for the day. The proprietor was taking down the shutters; we were his first customers.

The public room was skirted by an arboured terrace commanding a panorama of the city. We sat down at the end of a rustic table and ordered coffee and rolls to be brought to us out there. It was a pleasant spot, and the view was excellent. The sun was mounting a sky that was now free from clouds and presaged a grilling day, but a residue of the night's freshness tempered the morning air deliciously. Loud voices heralded the arrival of some workmen—white-coated bricklayers, their assistants in blue, plaster-spotted overalls, milkmen in tall caps with glossy leather peaks—who came for a glass of spirits or a coffee laced with rum. None of them showed any surprise at seeing us; in the free commune of Montmartre absolute equality reigns among the citizens. These people seemed quite satisfied with life. From the city spread at our feet rose one great purr of pleasure.

But my mind was overcast with a dull depression —the depression I had brought away with me from Mass. The angelic figure of the kneeling girl in the white velvet cloak had failed to oust the image of the evil-omened paupers. And I still saw that living reproach, the great despairing Christ in the midst of his perpetual Candlemas, as though in the ruddy glow of a conflagration. I said to Perbal:

"I'm uneasy. I'm terribly distressed by what I feel is going to happen. That's why I've been longing to see you—you always give me such encouragement."

"I feel worried, too," said Perbal. "I think I showed it yesterday evening, when we parted. Yes, even over there. . . ."

He lowered his voice as he always did when he spoke to me about his life abroad.

"Even there . . . where I'm the master . . . I think I can hear the preliminary cracking. Everything may be tottering! In any case, we've come to a terrible turning-point."

I continued:

"Are we on the verge of a huge upheaval, as our Jeremiahs say we are? I can't help thinking so at times. I have written about the end of the Roman world, the death-agonies of Latin Africa in the time of St. Augustine, and I seem to be experiencing the same mental anguish that rent civilization in the fifth century, on the eve of the great invasions.

Are we going to have another Barbarian Terror?"

We were silent for a time, not daring to express our thoughts completely, as if what we feared to acknowledge might hasten the catastrophe. Then, in a firmer tone, my friend replied:

"It's not only the barbarian terror that disturbs me. There are other terrors that attack the people of our time and are shared by every age . . . and not only every age of history but every age of life . . . they attack not only us old men who have only a few days more to live, but young people, even children. . . . Personally, I felt these terrors more keenly when I was twenty or so than at any other time. . . . Do you understand what I'm driving at? . . . The fear of growing old, the fear of suffering, the fear of death! . . ."

"I'm always thinking of it," I replied. "But there's no remedy for those misfortunes."

"I don't agree with you! I've been thinking very deeply about the matter, and I'm convinced that the remedy is there if we will only use it. We must not only accept the inevitable, but derive consolation from it. . . . Yes, we must find consolation, which is a state of peace, sometimes of well-being, perhaps even of happiness! . . ."

"But is it possible? Can one derive consolation from what is even more awful than loss of life itself: the necessity of living in the company of suffering, above all in the company of evil, moral evil? To live in evil, not merely pain, but in abjection, in subjection to evil—it's ghastly!"

"We must at least *try* to console ourselves. We

shall not be the first to have attempted it. Humanity has always thirsted after consolation, especially on the approach of universal crises, or when threatened by some vast upheaval. At Rome, during the convulsions of the Republic, during the tragic tyrannies of the Empire, and, later on, on the eve, or on the morrow, of the Invasions, consolation became quite a literary *genre*. Think of the works of consolation written by Cicero, Seneca, and Boethius. The *élite* of those days lived through worse times than we do. They lived under the threat of the sword; they were at the mercy of a capricious despot. They never knew when the door would open to admit the messenger of death. And what a death it was! As often as not its cruelty was enhanced by the most appalling tortures. Seneca's death was comparatively mild, but Cicero had his head cut off in a litter by a clumsy centurion, who spared him none of the horrors of execution. Boethius had his skull gradually crushed and his limbs torn off him on the rack. The executioners finished him off with clubs. In view of the possibility of such a fearful end, people took special steps to prepare themselves to meet it. They sought for antidotes to their terrors. There was a complete system of therapeutics to cure oneself of fear. Each ailment of the mind had its physician, its specialist. Seneca's *Epistles to Lucilius* were nothing more than a book of mental medicine to cure you of the fear of death. It was more than that: it was a panacea for every kind of ill—disease, disappointment, poverty, and so on. Later on, in the Middle Ages and afterwards, when the faithful looked on death as a fearful mystery, the number of consolers multiplied. And they seem to have found some efficacious remedies. Think of Philip II as he lay dying in his little cell in the Escorial. He had read to him the *Consolatio Pusillanimium* of the Benedictine, Louis de Blois—the little book that had consoled his father on his death-bed. . . ."

"But the disasters hanging over our heads are decidedly worse than anything that has been suffered in the past. If consolation is possible, as you say, the world has never been in greater need of it than now. . . ."

"Encouragement, too," put in Perbal, vigorously, "not just consolation. We must resist! It would be a disgraceful cowardice to resign ourselves to ignominy. Are we to accept defeat? Never! . . ."

And then, with sudden enthusiasm, he exclaimed:

"You must write a book on the subject—*The Book of Consolation* . . . and it must not merely be 'the cup of courage for the final agony' but the cordial to help one fight the good fight."

I fell silent, dismayed at his request and weighing in my mind the difficulty of the task. The silence was prolonged. Our eyes wandered over the city stretched below us, a city carried away by an insane desire for speed and noise, a victim to all the nerve-racking tumult of modern life—the monstrous fruit of a civilization which represents thousands of strivings and drudgeries, myriads of human brains frantically engaged in calculating, in inventing, in mitigating and embellishing our lives. . . .

"When all that has been destroyed," said Perbal, "when the stones of this basilica are buried beneath the grass, something must be permitted to survive: the tiny flame that will rekindle the extinguished hearths. . . . We mustn't shirk the question under the pretext of unworthiness. All of us, from the greatest down to the humblest, have the duty of nursing this tiny flame—the spark of future rebirth. . . ."

* * *

The book wrote itself. It was based on the talks I had with Perbal during his stay in Paris. We met about five o'clock every evening under the porch of the Basilica. We walked down the slopes of the Square Saint-Pierre and took a seat near the fountain, halfway down the hill, among the old people of the neighbourhood who were warming themselves in the setting sun, the housewives who gossiped together as they knitted, amid the squeals, the shrill cries, of children, that rose to our ears from the lower terraces. Our conversation was desultory, depending on casual suggestions and inspirations, without any pretence at being strictly logical; our only object was to study from every angle the questions that vitally concerned us. It was not till afterwards that I made any attempt to put our discussions into order. In addition, I have included all the views on the subject that are known to me, together with the results of my own reflection and the notes I have made when reading other authors.

PART I

OLD AGE

"Let us clasp old age to our bosom! Let us love it! It is full of comfort for those who know how to use it well."

SENECA
Epistles to Lucilius, XII.

"Close to the doorway side. . . . There the pale kin of Sickness dwells, and Eld, the woeful thing."

VIRGIL
Æneid, VI, 273–275 (tr. by William Morris).

CHAPTER I

THE IMMORTAL BEAUTY

IN October, after the summer spent in Paris with Perbal, I was invited to take part in a conference at Rome on the possibilities of a 'reconstruction of Europe'. On the day before I was due to return to France I was sitting in the deserted lounge of my hotel, writing letters, when the brisk tapping of heels on the tiled floor made me raise my eyes. A woman was coming towards me with short, rapid steps, apparently in search of someone. She seemed quite young, to judge from her lively gait and, still more, from her dress. Her appearance was vaguely familiar to me but I could not exactly place her. The question was settled by her suddenly bearing down on the table where I was writing and saying in a disdainful little voice:

"It's me all right! Don't look so worried!"

"Good Lord! I was wondering if it was you, Paulette. . . . Talk of the——"

I was on the point of saying something stupid, but she broke in smartly.

"How good of you to recognize me! The porter told me you were here, so I don't deserve any credit for recognizing *you*, but you——"

"I don't deserve any credit, either. You haven't altered in the least since we saw each other last

. . . ten years ago . . . do you remember? Outside the cathedral at Toledo. . . ."

"Oh, don't go into all that again, for Heaven's sake! People with memories get on my nerves. . . ."

There was a trace of impatience in the tone in which these last words were spoken. The woman, who, without any further ceremony, sat down in an armchair by my table, was a contemporary of mine, whom I had known in my childhood and in my youth . . . Paulette C., whom for the last half-century I had heard referred to as "*la belle Paulette*" and to whom I had given the additional title of "the Immortal Beauty," for her good looks, it appeared, were indestructible. For years she had been playing the part of a fashionable beauty acknowledged and proclaimed as such by the world at large . . . a professional beauty, one might say, though not in any derogatory sense, for Paulette is well-behaved and almost virtuous. She had never been known to have a lover. Her profession, her social usefulness, her work in the world, her *raison d'être*, her sole interest, is her beauty. Paulette was born beautiful and will die beautiful. She will do more than that: she will die 'young'—at ninety. . . .

In the fifty years that had passed since I first met her, hardly any alteration had taken place in her appearance. A blonde with violet-coloured eyes, she was—to me—still the same vision of loveliness that had dazzled my adolescence at the county balls. She seemed to be even livelier and perter now, with her stick, her short hair, her short skirt, and her perpetually restless little feet. I did notice, however, that her face had grown a little thinner, that its skin was showing minute cracks beneath the make-up, that its muscles seemed to be contracted, and that the whole mask had assumed a fixed, inanimate expression. Her beautiful fair hair, tinted to the roots, had lost its sheen, and from time to time she drew up her slim little body like a caryatid bowed down by some invisible weight. I noticed, too, that she carefully refrained from smiling, fearing, perhaps, to discompose her beauty. This gave her a rather tense expression of solemnity, that contrasted strangely with her natural frivolity. . . .

I said jocularly: "And to what do I owe the rare privilege of seeing you again? *Beato chi vi vede!*"

She put her finger to her lips. "That's a secret! . . . But don't worry, you'll soon know all about it!"

She was silent for a moment, and her expression grew more serious still. I thought of the crumbling beauty I had seen the day before, at Tivoli, and I thought to myself: How funny it is to see Paulette in Rome, the city of ruins!

She seemed to read my thoughts to some extent.

"Yes, Paulette in Rome! That's a surprise for you, isn't it? . . ."

I learnt later that she had come to obtain a nullity decree of her marriage, after at least forty years of married life. She was anxious, it appeared, to enter into a second matrimonial alliance, this time with a very young man who was neither good-looking, nor rich, nor clever, but with whom— no one knew why—she was hopelessly infatuated.

Paulette's husband was a gentleman, not much older than herself, who had given her no children but had loved her passionately for years. One of the innumerable grievances she had against him was that he had failed to make her happy. But who could claim the power of making Paulette happy? With her perpetual agitation, her instability of a little bird perched upon a twig, was she capable of a minute's happiness? Be that as it may, one fine day she declared that further living with her husband was intolerable—no matter how accommodating he might be—and she was about to commit the folly—at an unrevealable age—of throwing herself into the arms of a nit-wit!

"There's no need to tell you," she said, "that I've not come here to see museums. Some friends of mine brought me in their car. We are 'doing' Italy more or less haphazard. We've got no settled programme. . . . It's much jollier like that. . . . From here, as likely as not, we shall tear off to Vienna!"

"How young you are, Paulette!"

"I'm in the fashion, my dear, that's all! I always have been in it and I want to go on being in it till the end! . . . You're laughing at me. You think my 'youth' is all humbug! . . . Well, I don't want to be old! I don't know anything about old age; I hate it! I shall go on pretending till I'm done for! I shall keep whatever I can!"

As she spoke, a shadow seemed to pass across her eyes, as though she saw in front of her, with all its wrinkles and disfigurements, the Enemy she was fleeing, that old age the very mention of which appeared to cause her pain. Then suddenly her doll's face was lit up with a flash of rage.

"Old age? . . . I wish I could drive it off with a stick . . . a lipstick!"

I looked at her blood-red lips, her vermilion cheek-bones.

"Paulette," I said, "you've no need to drive it off. You're always twenty. You always will be twenty!"

"Ah, I don't care whether you laugh at me or not. It makes no difference. I'm like that. . . . Besides, you know I've got no brains. I'm worthless. Why do you waste your time talking to a worthless creature like me? How you must pity poor Paulette!"

"You misjudge yourself, Paulette. I know what you are. . . . Yes, I pity you, but for a different reason from the one you're thinking of. . . . To think that you could be so happy if you liked!"

"I don't want your happiness! . . . I must be up and doing! I must be on the move! I must amuse myself! That's the only way that life is possible for me! My husband bores me! . . . But they're calling me. I'll have to go. . . ."

A party of people in travelling attire were entering the lobby, and Paulette's name was being called.

"When shall I see you again?" I asked.

"Oh, not here, anyway. . . ."

"In Paris, then?"

"No, not in Paris, either. This trip's going to be a long one."

25

"All right, then, we'll meet in Heaven!"

She had already turned to go. Her friends were calling to her: "Hurry up, Paulette! We're late!"

Among the party which had come to fetch her was a young man—clearly the fiancé—who proceeded to cross-examine her in a loud, unpleasant voice—a false voice, ridiculously affected and pretentious, but one in which the tone of the master could already be discerned. . . .

* * *

And yet Paulette is no fool. She has good sense and judgement—for matters that have nothing to do with worldly conventions and the life she prides herself on leading. She has even a certain modicum of culture. When the mood takes her, she can read a serious book. She has an innate respect for intelligence, for great writers and their works, even for the classics. Coming from university stock, Paulette has a classical taste. When she likes, she can write a charming letter, full of witty, judicious, sometimes penetrating sayings. She has what is called 'good feeling', a certain quality of soul. But she seems to be ashamed of all this, as if to be sensible made her old.

She sneers at snobs, but she indulges in every kind of snobbery, in a fever of anxiety lest she fall behind the times. This *bourgeoise* proclaims herself to be a Bolshevist. This clever little person whose æsthetic taste stops short at 'The Broken Vase' or academic paintings, plunges headlong into every form of cubism and dadaism. She is convinced that this is what "keeps you young." And this respectable and, hitherto, virtuous wife, this sexagenarian who for years past has had no love for anything but her beauty, has taken into her head to have a gigolo, merely for the sake of posing as a little madcap. There was no need to upset her whole existence to gratify this desire; she could have done it with the full knowledge of her husband, who has long ceased to trouble himself about her goings-on. She is an unbeliever, not even practising her religion for the look of things. And yet she makes a great fuss about bringing her suit for nullity before the court of Rome, because she thinks it is the "thing to do," and because she imagines a second marriage will rejuvenate her. Anything rather than grow old!

* * *

Paulette will end as one of the troop of wretched crones who take refuge on the Côte d'Azur to hide their ridiculous obsession. Ruined by her fine friends, she will have no better retreat in her declining days than a family boarding-house. With a pitiful display of paint and powder she will parade the remnants of her wardrobe. She will moulder away in an attic in the Old Quarter of Nice, provided she is not found murdered in a bedroom of a questionable hotel or on a seat in the Promenade des Anglais. . . .

CHAPTER II

THE DISTRESS OF GROWING OLD

IT'S the same with all of us: we do not want to lose any of our past. We do not want to grow old. We too think we can stop the wheel of time. We cling to vain memories as though our very life depended on them.

A friend of mine is such a victim to this malady that he could not live without perpetually ruminating over his reminiscences. It is a deadly spell, a fatal fascination, that cripples every effort unconnected with the past. The least ray of sunshine that has flitted across his previous existence seems to him to be the focus of a blaze of light that must at all costs be rekindled. A street-corner in a country town evokes for him moments of youthful ecstasy, beyond which lies nothing. Even worse, the smell of a certain dish, the perfume of a wine, evoked by his imagination, dilates his soul. By hook or by crook he must recapture these moments, relive them. Without them life is nothing but a dreary waste; there is nothing left but death. And thus he fades away, dead already in his invalid's armchair, as he sits, chin in hand, eyes fixed anxiously on the fleeting visions that recede more and more irretrievably into the distance. . . .

There are moments, indeed, when one takes a

delicious pleasure in abandoning oneself to these mirages. But they are always as brief as they are deceptive. "Memory defrauds you. When you turn your head to look back on happiness it hides its crest in a mist of gold and seems to touch the skies, like the mountains, which, though they are actually no higher, prolong their shadows in the twilight."

We think we are regaining possession of ourselves; we are embracing shadows, the unconsciously created figments of our imagination.

Schopenhauer was well aware of this when he sought to define the soothing effect of æsthetic contemplation. "It is this bliss of contemplation, freed from the domination of the will, that casts over everything that is past or distant an illusive charm and presents these objects to us in a favourable light. *It is thus that we are our own deceivers*. When we recall the days—long since past—that we have spent in distant places, it is only objects that are evoked by our imagination, not the state of mind in which we were at the time and which, then as now, carried about with it its load of irremediable woes—woes which have been forgotten because they have since been frequently renewed. . . . Thus it is that the memory of past or distant scenes passes through our minds like the picture of a lost paradise. The imagination evokes only the objective, never the subjective or personal, part of our reminiscences. Consequently we imagine that this objective part was presented to us at the time quite pure, quite free from the unwelcome relations with the will,

[1] Flaubert, *Seconde Tentation de Saint Antoine*.

just as its image now presents itself to our fantasy. And yet the relations of these objects with our will caused us no less affliction then than now. . . ."

Only a little reflection is necessary to expose this fraud to the mind. But we revolt against the distressing conclusion that the past is lost beyond recall. With death in our soul we frantically endeavour to celebrate pretended joys that in reality are no more. We exhaust ourselves in prolonging the memory of them, even though we know quite well that this memory is only an illusion. This tantalizing little game cannot go on for long: it is agreeable provided only that it is not persistent. If it grows into a morbid habit it soon becomes intolerable. Remembrance becomes a torture: it is like the allegory conceived by D'Annunzio, the *Gavotte of the Ladies in Yellow*, the unforgettable dance of Ennui and Love. "Fair ladies who can no longer be described as young but who have barely left their youth behind them, clad in faded silk, the colour of yellow chrysanthemums, dance the gavotte with cavaliers dressed in pink. The latter, rather bored, bear in their hearts the picture of other, more beautiful, women—the flame of a new desire. The room in which they dance is over-large; its walls are lined with mirrors. The floor is parqueted with amaranth and cedar; from the ceiling hangs a great crystal lustre, with candles that are always about to be consumed and yet never are consumed. The women's lips, slightly drooping, are formed into a weak but everlasting smile. In the eyes of the cavaliers is an infinite ennui. A pendulum clock is always showing the same time; and the mirrors repeat and repeat the same movements over and over again. And the gavotte goes on and on, ever softly, ever slowly, ever smoothly, on and on, like the torture of love."

Those who are tormented by their memory are in a similar plight. Ennui is lying in wait for them. What their imagination brings back to them is not enough. They are compelled to delve, they are compelled to go ever further and further back. But the imagination tires. With the course of years the memory is exhausted; it loses colour. This is the "discoloration of ideas" that Loti speaks of, this infirmity of the memory that is said to affect mariners as well as the blind, when they stay too long out of sight of land.

* * *

To drive away old age with the aid of the memory is as futile, then, as driving it away with a lipstick. 'Pleasant memories' last but a few short moments and then only on condition that they are not too closely scrutinized. The Wheel of Time is stopped only by way of metaphor. My friend Paulette told me in Rome: "People with memories get on my nerves!"

Another friend, who has the Faith, writes to me as follows: "What a pity to paralyse oneself with memories, to lose one half of life while chewing the cud over the other! Away with memories! Let the dead bury their dead! Forward! Always forward! Away with the past! It no longer exists; it's a dead

weight; we must throw it off. It is nothing but
slavery and weakness, from which it is essential that
we free ourselves. Most of the time it is a *massa
peccati*, a mass of sin. Whatever is good in the past
is that which has no age, which sustains us now,
which carries us forward into the future. It is the
mainspring of our thought and action!"

With the oncoming of age action may be impossible; but thought remains intact, except in the
case of continual and intolerable suffering. It is the
function of thought to alter our views and in
rejuvenating itself to rejuvenate us. There comes a
time when thought turns against itself and life,
when it glimpses a way of salvation still untried.
Schopenhauer calls this turning-point "the conversion." We take exactly the reverse view of life to
that which we have taken hitherto; conversion is
life reversed, life with another goal, another inspiration. "For those who are still actuated by the will
(that is to say the will to live according to the
world), what remains, after the total suppression of
the will, is, in effect, nothing. Inversely, for those
who have converted and nullified the will, it is our
actual world, this real world, with all its suns and
all its Milky Ways, that is nothing. . . ."

Little by little there comes the settled conviction
that the sun of the dead is, in reality, the sun of
life, but a life so different from the one we know,
so alien to its essence, that it is the very contradiction of it.

This entry into a new world, this revelation of that
which cannot age—this is the great rejuvenation.

CHAPTER III

AN OLD MAN CONTENT
WITH HIS LOT

IN contrast to those who fly from old age and deny it, to those who undergo it with an invincible nostalgia for the past and with groans of despair, there are those who adapt themselves to it, who settle down to it, who even succeed in making it into a very comfortable little nest.

These last look on it solely as the time for retirement, as the period of life that is full of pleasures and—to use the ecclesiastical phrase—consolations. Viewed from afar by those in good health, old age takes on a poetic charm: there is something attractive about it. Mme de Maintenon, having performed her duty as a pedagogue by bringing up the bastard progeny of Louis XIV and Mme de Montespan, welcomed the arrival of the time for her retirement —a retirement generously provided for her by her grateful master. She wrote to her good-for-nothing brother: "I'm thinking of buying a place in the country. I've made an offer of 240,000 francs. Don't say anything about it yet. . . . I think we shall spend our old age very pleasantly, if such a thing be possible. . . ." In spite of her prudent qualification, it is clear that the wise Mme de Maintenon did not rule out the possibility of a pleasant old age. And Seneca, too, could write: "Let us clasp old age to our bosom! Let us love it! It is full of comfort for those who know how to use it well." For him it was the epitome of every kind of pleasure, the acme of delight, the moment that was all the more delicious in that it was the last. We must remember the charming, poetic ideas with which old age was envisaged by the ancients. Virgil dedicated some of his most beautiful verses to the Old Man of Tarentum who had the joy of gathering his vegetables from his garden, of tending his roses and his bees, and who in his modest ease felt as happy and as wealthy as a king. The type was so felicitous that a counterpart was considered necessary. Claudian matched the Old Man of Tarentum with his Old Man of Verona, who also had the pleasure of eating vegetables grown in his own garden and eggs laid by his own hens.

Lowly joys! . . . Are they sufficient to make old age supportable? Can we go further and say that it might be actually enjoyable?

* * *

However unlikely it may seem, this miracle sometimes comes to pass. I myself have known one of those fabulous old men celebrated by the poets. It was at Algiers, many, many years ago. We will call him the Old Man of the Bouzaréah, as he had a villa on the edge of the capricious road that winds its way interminably along the slopes of the hills of Bab el-Oued and Saint-Eugène, dominating the white terraces of the Kasbah, the port with its shipping, and the glittering curve of the bay, with the snowy Jurjura and the long chain of the Kabylian mountains in the distance. . . .

It is a delightful spot, verdant nearly all the year, an oasis of freshness in the alternately tepid or burning oven of the Sahel of Algiers. He had arranged his life there in the most judicious manner possible, with the most subtle knowledge of convenience, pleasure, and even beauty. And he enjoyed himself there to such an extent that he never wanted to leave the place: he was actually a Géronte [1] contented with his lot!

Everything had come his way: love, prosperity, even honours. He had no children, but he was surrounded by friends of his own choosing and young people with a future. His love for youth was no doubt prompted by the desire to enjoy the illusion of being young himself. It pleased him to direct or, if need be, reprimand these young associates of his. He liked to savour the joy of being superior to them by virtue of his experience, his practical wisdom. And as he was rich—as riches went in those days—the old man came in for a liberal amount of fuss and flattery. Everything was in his favour. No one, not even he himself, was in any doubt about his happiness.

* * *

At the time I knew him he was getting on for seventy.

[1] Géronte (from the Greek γερών) was the name of a character in early French comedy, typifying an old man.

35   D 2

He was a good-looking, jolly old fellow, with a well-knit, sturdy figure which he had kept in trim by continuing, despite his age, to indulge in sport. He had lived in Algeria since his youth; his life had been spent almost entirely out of doors, walking or riding in the mountains of Kabylia and across the Southern steppes. By the time I knew him he had been forced to abandon violent exercise, but he continued to live in the open air: he spent nearly the whole day out of doors. Every morning he played golf or tennis, always with the young of either sex. In the afternoon he went out walking or driving in his gardens, which covered a considerable area. This animal existence went to his head; he affected a boisterousness out of keeping with his years.

One day—either to impress or humiliate me—he took it into his head to run upstairs. He performed the feat nimbly enough but not without breathing hard. I can still see the painful effort of his long spine as it heaved up the remainder of his body, like an old draught-horse dragging a heavy load uphill.

On another occasion, at the end of dinner—to which he had done ample justice, in spite of incipient gout—I heard him exclaim: "I can do everything I did when I was twenty!"

And this is what he said, with a knowing wink, to some distant relatives of his who had an eye on his fortune and consequently overloaded him with flattering attentions: "I shouldn't be too sure, if I were you! I'm still capable of giving you some little cousins!"

In his youth he had enjoyed the successful love affairs to which his good looks more than entitled him. With a show of modesty he used to confess that as a ladies' man he must have been insufferably conceited. Having reached old age he imagined that he was free from all those trammels. But he was still susceptible to the charms of the other sex; and this susceptibility was the cause, if not of unacknowledged torments, certainly of a besetting preoccupation. It was the only sensitive spot in an existence that seemed to be completely halcyonic.

An admirer of Georges Sand and de Musset, whole passages from whose works he could quote at will, he prided himself on having indulged in romantic passion to the full. It was not quite certain who had inspired these tumultuous passions; all that was known was that he had been violently in love with his wife, whose beauty, so I was assured, was irresistible at the age of twenty. History—or legend—had it that he had ' carried her off' in the style of the romances of the Restoration period. Had there been a scaling of walls, a silken ladder, a swift horse galloping through the night, a cloak flapping in the wind? Those who recounted the adventure led one to conclude as much. . . . And then this sublime passion had died a natural death. The mediocrity of the creature who had been its object gradually dawned on the incorrigible lover.

She stayed on in his life like a pitiable waif whose presence was a torture not only to the unfortunate girl herself but also to everyone who was a witness of this irremediable rejection. Nevertheless he was always surrounded by women, who were tormented by secret jealousy. He could afford to be old; he lived on his reputation as a great lover, he trailed behind him the perfume of passion, and doubtless he bore the invisible mark of it on his brow—invisible, but immediately perceptible to those who are also marked with it. He went on being a charming man, a man who gives pleasure to others —one does not know exactly why—and always will give pleasure; the sort of man who is spoken of as 'a splendid fellow' and will continue to be spoken of as such until he is ninety at least. A swarm of foolish women buzzed round him like wasps round a cluster of late autumnal fruit.

Among these hopeless lovers was one who was so pathetic that I can never think of her without being moved to pity. She was an elderly spinster, about the same age as Géronte. She came of a family of high officials which was on intimate terms with my friend's family, and she had known him when he was quite a child. They had played together, and naturally she had lost her heart to him. She had always loved him, with a love which had become more concentrated and more jealous with the passing of the years. She was quite small, quite insignificant, quite pitiful, and always languishing— a rather comic contrast with the jovial, handsome Géronte, the object of her adoration, who pretended to be oblivious of this silent passion. The little old woman was always dressed in black, with a simple garden-hat trimmed with black ribbon, as if she

were in perpetual mourning for her hopeless love·
Her name was Blanche. I mention this only because
the name Blanche went so extraordinarily well with
her pale face, the pallor of her whole person and
her whole existence.

Although she was not well off—she was entirely
dependent on a meagre income—she had not
hesitated to cross the water and to take up her
abode in Algiers, when her friend took up his abode
there. This had happened nearly forty years before
I knew her. She had followed him so as not to be
robbed of the joy of keeping him in sight. For forty
years she had been living in what was little better
than a native hut, only a few paces from her idol's
villa. All this time, without the slightest hint of a
reproach, without the slightest allusion to her love,
she had been the tortured witness of his happiness.
He, out of pity, allowed her to enjoy his company.
The dear creature gave such little trouble, she was
so discreet! She took up such little room! But when
the idolized wife had ceased to please, she was too
proud to join the frivolous swarm of idolizers. She
had prevailed on her beloved to set aside a special
day for her, for her alone, as a reward for her long,
dumb fidelity. Once a week she had the right to
enjoy his company; on the other days she lived on
the memory of it. Ah! how she relished those hours
in which he was really present! What bliss! A whole
evening with the husband and the abandoned wife!
What could they have had to say to one another,
those two forsaken women, in front of the man who
showed them every politeness, every deference, but

39

who firmly declined to encourage their affection?

He considered himself very generous, very magnanimous to both of them. He made them feel the value of his favour, and the poor little old woman guarded it fiercely. If an unexpected visitor happened to break in on the privacy of the trio, she was furious. She was incapable of concealing her vexation. Géronte smiled at it in his beautiful grey beard, and to maintain his affability to the bitter end he would gallantly introduce her to the intruder as "My young friend Blanche P——!"

It was a most distressing joke. The "young friend" was made to look as though she might be the aunt or mother of her ever-young contemporary. . . . On such occasions she would leave the party, rising with a tired and woebegone expression, and return, alone, to her dreary lodging, wearing her black-ribboned hat and her narrow shawl. The superb Géronte, who sometimes exercised his gallantry so far as to escort her through the garden in the darkness, never wondered whether it was any lighter in the heart of his "young friend Blanche P——" . . .

* * *

In addition to his physical advantages, the septuagenarian was possessed of a fairly substantial fortune.

Although for some time past he had been enjoying a regular income from investments, his life was by no means an idle one. He had been in business, and he still continued to dabble in it to some extent. He presided at board meetings, pocketed his director's fees, bought and sold, and went in for building, both on his own account and others'. Like Louis XIV, he had a mania for building.

As a result of his mania he had succeeded in embellishing his villa—which, when he inherited it from his parents, was an unpretentious little building—to a remarkable degree. He was not by any means a Crœsus—in fact, his means were definitely limited—but he managed to provide himself with more than comfort; he was able to enjoy the illusion of extreme luxury, even of art and beauty. Flaubert used to tell his friends that he would need thousands of millions of francs to satisfy all his wishes and his tastes; Géronte succeeded in doing so at a far less cost.

It was a luxury easily obtained: he had a great love for flowers, like the Old Man of Tarentum. In spring, and even during most of the winter, his gardens were wonderful. The plants themselves were nothing out of the ordinary, but he arranged them and set them out with the greatest possible effect. Then again, though he had had no architectural training, he himself designed the elevations of his buildings. He used only common materials, the outlay was only moderate, yet some of his results were very charming. The way he adapted the Moorish *patio* to the demands of European taste and comfort was most ingenious. The drawback about the *patio* is the feeling of confinement that it gives you, with its four walls completely blocking out the view. He had the happy notion of opening

his on the east side, thus obtaining a splendid view
of the sea and mountains. The three remaining
sides, which he furnished with arcades, caught the
sun and provided a series of rooms open to the air.
There was a perpetual murmur of fountains and
running water in the *patio*. He had even set up a
kind of antique fountain such as wealthy Romans
used to have in their *triclinia*. It consisted of a slab
of marble enlivened with arabesques and furrowed
with a maze of little zigzag channels, so that the
sound of the water, returning on itself, modulated
its song more softly. . . .

Having tired of the annual trip to France made
by most Algerians who have the necessary means, he
arranged his villa so as to be able to live through the
torrid African summer with a minimum of discomfort. He built himself a covered swimming pool in
the style of the Moorish baths. A judicious amount
of daylight was allowed to filter through the pierced
roof of the *kubba* on to the marble basins and the
white surfaces of the walls and paving, which were
variegated by brilliantly coloured mats and the
large green leaves of arums and hibiscus. It was
delicious, on a blazing hot afternoon, after a siesta
on a couch in a shady, airy recess, to plunge into
the pool and "enjoy the ecstasy of water," as
Géronte used to say. He indulged himself in this
pleasure every day, in spite of his seventy odd years.

In the dog-days, when the heat was too intense,
he moved to Chréa, where he had built himself a
chalet at the summit of the mountain, six thousand
feet above the sea. He found there the traces of

snow, frozen wind that had passed across the Mediterranean, and the double azure of the bay and sky. . . .

* * *

This modern Epicurean positively radiated happiness; he was the embodiment of optimism—the effervescent sort. He was a veritable apostle of bliss. He took great pains to give pleasure, so as to be surrounded by smiling faces. This is not to say that he was kind—in the fundamental sense. Without exactly being the contrary, he cultivated a pretty egoism that brooked no interference. He must have been very hard in business, and he was still a redoubtable adversary, but so as to play a pretty rôle before his conscience, with a sort of moral coquetry he was anxious to have a reputation for being kind. On occasions he really wanted to be kind. "Magnanimity" was a hobby-horse of his; the word was constantly on his lips; and this sometimes rendered him capable of a certain self-sacrifice for others. Now and then he was willing to be of service, even of benefit, to his fellow-men, provided that he was not unduly inconvenienced thereby. He was not disposed to put himself out for anybody; it ran contrary to his habits and, one might even say, his æsthetic sense and his idea of life. He had, accordingly, no qualms in inflicting on his wife as well as his "young friend Blanche P——" the presence of his admiring females, although he was well aware that it tortured both of them. He paid no heed to this, since, in his

43

opinion, he was doing all that could reasonably be expected of him in giving the former all the comforts that wealth provides, the latter the joy of feasting her eyes upon his person. He considered that he was behaving very gallantly in the matter.

Encouraged by the general admiration he received, he regarded himself as a superior being, as an artist. When showing people round his gardens and his buildings he would say: "I create beauty!" very much as Clemenceau used to say "*Je fais la guerre!*"

In his youth he had published his slim book of verse and even a novel, and on the strength of this he criticized the poor tribe of writers from a lofty height. He had known all the theatrical and literary stars; he spoke of them familiarly as of old acquaintances, long forgotten. Being thus quite certain of his worth, content with himself and with those around him, content with fortune and with life, he steeped himself in a bath of perpetual self-content. And this maintained him in a state of well-being. He wished well to the whole human race—and in his moments of exaltation, while displaying the utmost scepticism, he would be so far carried away as to render thanks to "the Unknown Cause" which had made the world so beautiful. . . .

* * *

Having thus settled his existence once and for all, he arrived at extreme old age without having met with any great vexation. He became, in the full sense of the term, the Old Man of the Bouzaréah. In the twilight of his fading years he was in luck's way again in finding the ideal nurse. His wife dead, his friends either dead or scattered, he might well have contemplated with terror a life of solitude, all the more cruel in view of the number of admirers who had previously kept him company and flattered him. He might have fallen into mercenary hands and, in spite of the good wages paid, have been badly cared for and badly assisted at his last moments. But it seemed as if Fortune were in love with him, as if she, too, dogged his footsteps. A devoted, intelligent, and affectionate nurse kept him company at his bedside until the very end. Though infirm and impotent, no longer able to spend more than a few hours daily out of bed, he retained his mental clarity and his cultivated tastes intact, continuing to enjoy his books, and still appreciative of the beauties of the landscape and the magnificent displays of Nature. In fact, it was generally agreed that Fortune was as favourable to him towards the end as she had been all along. For him, old age was perhaps the happiest season of his life.

* * *

The obvious retort to this would be: "But that case was exceptional. People don't often die as happily as that." But the thing is not so rare as one might think. A neighbour of mine at Nice, the painter Chéret, died at the age of ninety-six in full possession of his faculties, as the saying goes, and with his taste for life unspoilt, although he had gone completely blind some years before his death . . . and blindness was, perhaps, for him, something even more cruel than paralysis was for the Old Man of the Bouzaréah. Well, Chéret continued to get about and to take an interest in matters that affected his profession, in literature, in scientific discoveries, the theatre, and politics. Just before he died he came downstairs and rested in the garden, and at the very last he said quite simply to the person who was looking after him: "This is the end. I'm going."

He did in fact go before the day was out. He had never once complained—an almost incredible phenomenon in the case of one who has lost his sight, especially if he has been an artist passionately in love with all the bright and joyful forms of life, a man who had taken a voluptuous delight in colour.

These are recent cases; the list would be a long one were I to add to it the classical examples of old men who have retained to the end, not only their intellectual faculties, but a robust health and even an aptitude for pleasure—from Massinissa, who, when he was nearly a hundred, continued to throw the javelin and spent whole days in the saddle, to the Maréchal de Richelieu, who married, for the third time, at the age of eighty-four.

And how about those ancients of both sexes who positively refuse to die, who bury their children, their grandchildren, and their great-grandchildren, and as the sole survivors of a complete generation long since disappeared, flaunt themselves on a pile of coffins as if deriding youth? . . . I have in mind an old woman well known in the world of letters, who had been an explorer in her youth and was still an indefatigable traveller at ninety-six. She was just as much a sportswoman as she always had been, she was always the first arrival at hotels, always the first at table, and invariably secured for herself the best bedroom, the best seat in the carriage, the best cabin. At a stopping-place on an expedition you would find her with a cigarette between her lips, seated at a table with a glass of port or a cup of tea in front of her, while the rest of the party were still toiling along the dusty road. Alpenstock in hand, cleaving the air like a figure-head, amid a swirl of fluttering gauze, she would stride briskly down the mountain-paths, followed by a footsore and broken-winded band of young companions.

* * *

Still, it must be admitted that these prolongations of youth are exceptions to the rule and that they constitute, as it were, a defiance of the law of Nature. And are they really as happy as they are represented? Is euthanasia so simple and so easy? . . . I should be curious to know if Géronte, nailed to his bed by gout and paralysis in his villa on the Bouzaréah, still continued to view the world and existence through rosy spectacles. This *bon viveur* must have had some terrible moments, apart from the final agony. And when Chéret said to those around him: "This is the end. I'm going!" with

47

every outward sign of perfect calm, who knows what may have been passing through his mind at this supreme instant, what may have been the real significance of this final glimmering of consciousness?

Besides, a thousand artifices are necessary to maintain the aged in a state of happiness such as these two men may be presumed to have enjoyed. It presupposes a certain degree of material prosperity, together with assiduous, meticulous, and complicated attention on the part of others. Interest is concentrated on one's body and one's health. And it takes for granted, above all, a state of social calm, order, security, contentment of the lower classes, respect for the prosperity of others, and no sign of Communism or Bolshevism in the offing. In other words, a time of peace and plenty, a golden age that comes once, perhaps, just to show us how impossible it is.

At the end of every life there comes the cup of bitterness and in most cases, preceding its arrival, a period of decrepitude and suffering too great to be treated with contempt.

The ancients, who were exposed to more distress than we are, worked out a complete system of reasoning to help them make this critical and painful passage as comfortably as possible. But how much is this system worth? Can it be put to any use by us mortals of today? . . .

CHAPTER IV

THE WISDOM OF THE ANCIENTS

THE ancients had regular "Schools for Old Men."

In their days one learnt how to grow old gracefully as one learnt how to die. Professional philosophers set up shops of wisdom; they taught and practised a complete system of therapeutics to counteract old age. The teaching was more or less the same in all the schools that enjoyed the patronage of the public. The two most popular sects—the Epicureans and the Stoics—may have differed on the question of principle, but they were at one when it came to practical morals. Their moral laws, transmitted and perpetuated by generations of exponents, underwent hardly any alteration in the course of centuries. Although Seneca belonged to a different school from that of Cicero, his ethics were practically the same, at any rate as regards the fundamental questions of life, death, old age, virtue, and the highest good, and it is practically certain that Cicero had broken no new ground but had confined himself to repeating the lessons he had learnt from his Greek preceptors.

To Cicero we are indebted for the most complete extant treatise on old age—his *De Senectute*—which was written more or less in honour of the elder

A.S.   49   E

Cato, who, in the minds of the Romans of that time, was the ideal of a gentleman grown old: the man of practical common sense who knows how to protect and increase his property, attains to every public honour without creating a commotion in the process, and finally serves his country as well as he has served his heritage . . . the man of action, who in his old age develops virtue and becomes a man of thought. Cicero does not conceal that fact that, just as Plato had idealized Socrates, so he, too, has somewhat idealized the wily veteran, who, at bottom, was nothing more than a greedy peasant whose virtue consisted mainly in conducting his affairs with profit and in holding fast to the customs of his ancestors.

In *De Senectute* Lælius and Scipio Æmilianus are represented as paying a visit to the worthy Cato at his country house. After a brief preamble they address him thus:

"We hope—at least we wish—to become old. You would be doing us a great favour by teaching us the easiest way of supporting the burden of increasing years."

Note that the interview presumably took place at Tusculum, a stone's throw from Cicero's villa, in view of lovely mountain scenery, but no mention is made of this in the dialogue, although the old gentleman makes numerous allusions to his gardens and his orchards and speaks of his vines and his bees in an almost lyrical strain. For the ancients as for the present-day Moslems and other peoples that have remained ingenuous, Nature was by no manner of means an object of contemplation. They liked it only for its pleasures and the conveniences or commodities it provided. They looked to it to supply them with shade, fresh air, running water, fruit for the table, wood for heating. The sight of it gave them nothing but the satisfactory feeling of proprietorship. The sprouting of the crops, the opening of the buds, interested them merely on account of the material profits they foretold. . . .

The conversation was held only a few miles from Tivoli. If its participants had gone on to the Temple of the Sibyl they would have derived no pleasure, as I did, in watching the waterfalls at the Villa d'Este and the fountain-jets as tall as the aged cypresses. They go straight to the subject that for them is a question of the greatest urgency: old age. Is there an art of growing old? Is there a remedy for decay? . . .

* * *

To begin with, old people must be amiable, especially with the young. They must 'make up' to them, live with them as much as possible, be present at their games, and, as Montaigne says in paraphrasing Plato, try to take an interest in them, "so as vicariously to rejoice in the suppleness and beauty of the body, which is no longer theirs, and to recall in their memory the grace and comeliness of that verdant age. . . ."

They must present a smiling visage:

"Amiable, indulgent old men spend their declining days comparatively happily, whereas the man of embittered and regretful temperament is miserable at every period of his life." We must even try to be handsome old men, pleasing to the eye, carefully dressed, not slovenly, ugly, unsavoury dotards who scare away the young and depress even their contemporaries. In addition, those who are ageing ought to make up their minds once for all to yield to Nature. Nature does not want us to do at seventy what we used to do at twenty. Each period of life has the pleasures and the occupations that beseem it. When judged dispassionately, old age is not entirely unattractive. Let us see how this is so.

According to Cato—or rather Cicero, who makes Cato his mouthpiece—"There are four considerations that make old age appear to the majority of men to be a deplorable catastrophe. Firstly, it causes us to retire from business. Secondly, it makes the body more and more infirm. Thirdly, it deprives us of almost every physical pleasure. Fourthly, it is in close proximity to death."

There is no denying this fourth consideration, but are the other three entirely true? And if so, are they true for everybody?

* * *

First of all, exactly what sort of business is meant? Private or public? But in any case, elderly men are excellently suited for either, says Cato. "Those who deny that old men are capable of conducting business are over-hasty in their judgement. They are like the man who said that a pilot on board ship is good for nothing because he stays quietly in the stern, tiller in hand, while the crew are either climbing to the mast-heads or are busy on deck or are emptying the bilge. The occupations of old age are not the same as those of youth, but they are preferable and more important. Serious business is not transacted by means of force, agility, or speed, but by prudence, authority, and sound judgement, all of which qualities, far from being absent in old age, are found there in a superior degree. Perhaps you think that I, who have been engaged in various kinds of warfare as private, captain, general, and commander-in-chief—am no longer of any use? But it is I who instruct the Senate as to the wars it ought to wage, and how it ought to wage them. . . ."

And Cato proceeds with pride to remind his listeners that it was he in fact who had brought about the overthrow of Carthage, Rome's great rival. Old as he was then, he had exercised a decisive influence on the fortunes of his country. In reality, old age was ideal for politics. Practical wisdom was never more acute than when it was founded on the experience of a lifetime.

* * *

It may be said, perhaps, that human powers have their limit, as they have their decline! It is depressing to see an orator or a statesman losing more and more of his physical and intellectual vigour. It is inevitable that his lungs should tire, that his voice should lose its resonance, that his memory should grow dim.

But these failings can be remedied. The memory, like the voice, weakens because it is no longer exercised. We must fight against this enfeeblement with all our might. By dint of daily exercise the voice can be maintained in all its vigour, in the same way as the musician preserves the suppleness of his fingers. The memory is in similar case. Among other methods that of the Pythagoreans should be adopted: every night, before falling off to sleep, they go over in their minds all that they have done, seen, heard, or learnt, during the day.

Even though the memory fails with the passing of the years, the other faculties, such as reasoning powers, judgement, perspicacity, and general intelligence, not only remain intact but are actually increased. It certainly seems, however, that in the case of the artist, the poet, the dramatist, and the narrator, their creative powers gradually diminish. The probable cause of this is that this faculty belongs to some extent to the animal part of human nature. Mimicry, which constitutes the essence of a work of art, belongs to the physical sphere. But exceptions to the rule—if it is a rule—are numerous. Sophocles was ninety when he wrote the *Œdipus Coloneus*, one of his finest tragedies. Simonides, Stesichorus, Pindar, and other lyric poets composed their best odes at an advanced age. And has not posterity always conceived Homer as a patriarch? His two great poems are considered to be the fruit of an almost divine antiquity.

But let us admit that these are exceptions and that the creative genius does diminish as the years roll on. On the other hand, in what fine fettle the other faculties may be maintained! Plato was still teaching when he was almost a centenarian. The same may be said of Zeno and Cleanthes. Study, intellectual work of any kind, is always possible, provided that we do not allow ourselves to become slack or rusty. We must work, and go on learning. Cato cites himself as an example; he began to study Greek when he was well advanced in years and it was then that he wrote his *Origines*, his treatises on the *Rights of Augurs*, the *Rights of Pontiffs*, and *Civil Rights*. . . . The dying Socrates wanted to learn the lyre, simply for the sake of knowledge, for the beauty of the thing. . . .

These kinds of occupation do not require the strength of an athlete, which, in any case, would be useless to the old; on reaching the age of seventy, one no longer has the inclination to run races in the stadium or to throw the javelin, though it is true that some old men retain their youthful vigour to the last. "You have heard, of course, about Massinissa, who has now reached his ninetieth year. If he undertakes a journey on foot he never mounts a horse. If he sets out on horseback he never leaves the saddle. No matter how wet or cold it is, he always goes bareheaded. His body is free from every infirmity, and consequently he is always in a fit condition to fulfil all the duties and ceremonies of royalty. . . ."

This case, too, is an exception. But we need not

argue about the body; it is only natural that the older it grows the feebler it becomes. The spirit, however, triumphs over it if the proper therapeutic method is adopted: "We must brace ourselves against old age and correct its weaknesses with care. We must resist it as we resist disease. Firstly, we must pay attention to our health, take a moderate amount of exercise, and eat and drink only as much as is necessary to repair, not overtax, our strength. Then—the most important point of all—we must nourish our minds and our senses. . . . The mind should be kept as taut as a bow, in no way allowed to fail or languish. . . . Absorbed as I am in my studies and my work, I have little opportunity to regret my loss of bodily strength. I visit my friends. I frequently attend the Senate. I bring before it plans that have been long and deeply pondered. And even were I incapable of doing this I should enjoy myself on my couch, reflecting on matters which I could not personally carry into execution. But I have retained the faculty of doing so, thanks to the active life that I have always led. In this manner one grows old little by little without taking cognizance of the fact, and instead of being struck down at a single blow one simply passes away by dint of living."

* * *

The chief complaint that can be brought against old age is that it deprives us of a host of physical pleasures, in particular those of love.

We ought rather to be thankful for the fact.

56

Voluptuousness is the enemy of reason; old age frees us from it. It liberates us from the bondage of the flesh; it delivers us from a hard and tyrannical master, who metes us out more torments than delights. "We ought to welcome old age inasmuch as it frees us from the ardent desire of any kind of pleasure." As for the pleasures of love, old age ceases eventually to have any desire for them at all. Sophocles, on being asked whether he still enjoyed these pleasures, replied: "May the gods preserve me from them! I gave them up as willingly as I would have quitted a savage and infuriated master. For those who have been eagerly desirous of these things the deprivation of them may be gall and wormwood, but for one who is fully sated, the deprivation of them is preferable to their enjoyment—if we may apply the term 'deprivation' to the absence of something for which one has no desire whatever. . . ."

Old age has other pleasures and, if need be, consolations. The pleasures of the mind, which become keener with age, are supreme, but life leaves us plenty of others to be gleaned, for instance those of the table and of conversation. The latter is the chief delight of aged folk; nothing gives them greater pleasure than to have a chat—not that this prevents them from tasting the delights, with a moderation befitting their years, of a good cuisine. "Certainly," declared the venerable Cato, "I highly approve of the custom instituted by our forefathers of appointing presidents of the feast, and the speeches delivered by the president, cup in hand, as was the custom in our parents' time. Like Xenophon, in his *Banquet*, I too am very fond of quaffing those slight draughts that merely wet the gullet, either in front of a good fire or in the sun, in winter, or in the shade in summer. This is how I live in my country house amid the Sabine Hills; I have a regular feast with my neighbours every day, and in discussing various subjects we prolong these meetings as far into the night as possible. . . ."

* * *

Then there are the pleasures of being a farmer and proprietor.

With what feeling, with what accents of devotion, of gratitude, to the earth that provides him with them, does the shrewd old peasant describe these pleasures!

"It is not merely the earth's fruits that please me, but also its nature and its virtue. It is always obedient to the hand that governs it, and whatever it receives it never fails to return with interest. . . . Consider the planting, the sprouting, the spreading of the vine! . . . Do you see its tendrils? They are, as it were, its hands, grasping everything that seems to offer itself for the purpose. To prevent it exhausting itself in superfluous shoots the dresser skilfully plies his knife among the multitude of roving branches. And then, in the spring, the buds appear on the stock that has been left, and in the joints of the branches. The buds soon develop into leaves and clusters. The grape expands, fertilized by the

58

moisture of the earth and the warmth of the sun. It is bitter to the taste at first but becomes sweeter as it ripens and, under the protection of the foliage, enjoys a gentle warmth without exposure to the scorching sun. Is there anything more cheerful, more beautiful, than the vine-plant with its foliage and fruit? . . . But I could never weary of telling you about the recreations and delights of my old age! . . ."

The country is where one ought to spend the evening of one's life. Not only is the air there better for the aged, not only will they find tranquillity, and food and surroundings appropriate to their time of life, but the country is the preserver of all the domestic virtues; it protects the dignity of their life.

All the great ancestors, the true fathers of the nation, the great soldiers, the great statesmen, were first of all peasants who began by grasping the handle of the plough.

* * *

Nevertheless, the fact cannot be insisted on too often: old age is not, in itself, a state of blessedness. Far from it! Wrinkles and grey hairs do not necessarily entail either good health, prudence, wisdom, honours, or contentment. A perfect old age is the fruit of a well-spent, active, hard-working, temperate, intelligent, and virtuous life. This is the price that must be paid if we wish to spend our last few years contentedly. This will ensure respect for age, this will ensure the honours that come spontaneously.

"Although it may seem an unimportant, trivial matter in itself, it is very pleasing to our self-respect to see how people greet us, come to meet us, make way for us, rise at our approach, escort us from place to place, and come to consult us. . . . In our Senate the eldest augurs are given precedence even over the dignitaries vested with supreme authority. What corporal delights could be compared with such flattering prerogatives as these?"

And Cato, carried away by enthusiasm for his age, is emboldened to make the following frank disclosure of his inmost thoughts: "If the world consisted solely of the aged, we should all live far more comfortable and judicious lives. Old people are intelligent, reasonable, and prudent. No State could exist without them. . . . They are the foundation of the public weal."

This is a long cry from the modern slogan of *"Giovinezza! Giovinezza!"* The descendants of Curius and Cato have reversed the policy of their ancestors.

* * *

The final objection to old age—and it is a vital one—is its proximity to death.

There is no denying the truth of this, but the answer to it is that "death is just as near to the young as to the old." Every period of life is equally exposed to it. It is the common lot. But as though he realized that the argument is unreal, the author turns to other consolations. I have in mind especially the feeling of consolation that the old must have in looking back on a life well spent and in saying to themselves: "I have not been born in vain!" The most potent, and possibly the only valid, argument is, for those who are far advanced in years, the feeling that they have had enough of life. This wise renunciation should be the fruit of old age just as a happy old age is the fruit of a worthy life. There comes a moment when, quite naturally, we feel ripe for departure. We detach ourselves from existence just as the fruit detaches itself from the tree. We have oldened gradually and imperceptibly. We are not suddenly broken off; "*we die by dint of having lived*."

And then there is the hope of being reunited with our friends, with those who are dear to us. The intercourse begun beneath the olive trees of Tibur will be continued beneath the myrtles of the Elysian Fields. And with this promise for the future the sage eagerly intones his Farewell Song: "I not only want to meet my personal acquaintances but also those about whose noble deeds I have either heard, or read, or written. When the day comes for me to go, it will be difficult to keep me back. I should have no desire to regain my youth, like Pelias. Were some deity to offer me the chance of going back from old age to childhood, of puling again in swaddling clothes, I should certainly refuse it! . . . O glorious day when I shall leave for that celestial assembly, the divine council of souls, the day when I shall be quit of this terrestrial rabble, this terrestrial slime! . . . That is why, O Lælius, O Scipio, old age sits light upon me!"

These are about the most important, or at any rate the best, consolations that the wisdom of the ancients has to offer to the aged.

The pagan moralists did nothing more than resume and develop these themes; they made no original contributions. The only thing approaching novelty that I could find was the remark of Seneca's that old age gave the savour of life its supreme bouquet. He has also hit upon some pretty similes by way of illustration: "Fruits are more sought after the further the season advances, and youth grows more beautiful as it draws towards its end. Topers find more pleasure in the last draughts they drink, in the last gulp that souses them and puts the finishing touch on their drunkenness. Each pleasure reserves to the end what is most intense. . . ."

All this is very charming and doubtless highly consolatory, but does it console? Your moderns may come to the conclusion that in this matter the ancients were not *difficile*, or exigent. But have they discovered anything more satisfactory? . . .

CHAPTER V

A MODERN COMMENTARY

OLD age, which at no time has been seen as attractive, has never been more discredited than it is today. It is not merely prejudice, it is actual hostility, or even hatred. Hitherto, such an attitude has been found only among a few savage and extremely backward races. As a rule, the elderly male members of a tribe are supposed to be the guardians of either dangerous or useful secrets, and for this reason they are feared or tolerated, as the case may be. Among modern civilized folk, old age has lost every semblance of prestige. Its reputation for wisdom has disappeared. Elderly people are either emasculated, feeble-minded, or completely imbecile. They are mischievous, malicious, and capable of any scurvy trick. They thirst after youthful blood. It is not only anti-militarists who denounce with disgust those whom they are pleased to call "bloodthirsty old men"; Bolshevists and Communists also regard them as useless mouths which it were best to suppress or let starve. What is more, aged people are reactionaries who obstruct or retard the march of revolution. It is more expeditious to get rid of them altogether than to argue with them.

The animal jealousy between the different ages has been systematized into a doctrine which has been put at the service of the lowest revolutionary instincts. It means the general mobilization of youth, not only against generations that are dead and gone, and which, at the worst, are detestable and absurd, but against the generations that have immediately preceded it and are still alive. The contempt with which young Hitlerites speak of the aged must be heard to be believed. There is no question of maintaining that intelligence is the exclusive privilege of the old; but how alarming are those governments that throw on the scrap-heap, along with bourgeois intelligence and culture, the moderating wisdom of maturity, and which end by ruling out of court both mind and soul! And all this for what is known to them as 'dynamism', in other words brute force. Michelet violently stigmatizes this kind of government in his *Bible de l'Humanité*. "The military orgy of Alexander and his successors was followed by the plebeian orgy of the Cæsars, the apotheosis of the trooper by the apotheosis of the brute." It seems to me that this is what is happening to us. . . .

Most of us have heard the story about the ambassadors from Sparta who were attending a play at Athens and rose from their seats to give place to an old man. . . . Nowadays, no one— stripling or ambassador—gives up his seat to any-one, not even in a motor-bus, not even to an old lady.

* * *

The therapeutic measures employed by the ancients against old age were essentially spiritual.

Our methods and remedies are essentially material. Whereas they devoted their attention first and foremost to the soul, using every means to forearm it and fortify it against the afflictions of old age, our treatment is almost entirely confined to doctoring the body. We aim at prolonging the vigour of the aged; we hold out hopes to them of a complete rejuvenation. And what wonderful attempts have been made in this direction! They have been noisily advertised, and their claim to produce definite results has been received with acclamation. Think of the salt-water treatment introduced by René Quinton! And the graftings, and the injections of regenerating sera! How agreeable and convenient it would be if we could thus rejuvenate ourselves at will! . . . A propos of this, I have a letter from one of my medical friends in which he says: "One of my patients has had a grafting operation performed upon him at the age of sixty-five. First of all, he was laid up with fever for several weeks, and when he had got over that he was even weaker and more lifeless than before. All these so-called remedies are ineffectual!" The disillusionment is complete. Yet I could wish my friend's opinion mistaken or at least exaggerated! Not that I am anxious to prolong my life, but so that all the sufferings of old age might be checked or shortened.

It would be going too far, then, to say that old men are a thing of the past, but the claim is put forward with assurance as regards old women. The beauty parlours have set everything to rights. 'Elderly spinsters' have disappeared; no woman now is older than she looks. By means of judicious massage and stitches cleverly concealed by the hair, wrinkled skins are stretched taut and firmness is re-imparted to the flesh. A woman's face can be repaired almost as effectively as a piece of cracked china or a broken plate. I know of some sexagenarian women who have succeeded in preserving the freshness of their complexion and the elasticity of their epidermis, or, rather, they appear to have done so—at a distance. But in spite of it all people go on dying just the same. Youth, it seems, can be prolonged, but not life itself. Every step forward in the path of progress, every medical discovery, seems to provoke a crop of new diseases and a recrudescence of the old. Heart disease and appendicitis have never been so common as they are today. Moreover, do all these artificial methods of rejuvenation prevent us from experiencing the ravages of time, its degradation, its disgrace? We are only too conscious of our age, and that is enough to poison the soul, unless we resign ourselves to the situation.

Why not simply accept the necessity of growing old? Why go on dressing like a flapper when one is more than old enough to be a grandmother? . . . In *Le Temps d'Aimer*, by Gérard d'Houville, there is a charming portrait of an old lady who not only acknowledges her age but seems to want to make it as agreeable as possible by careful attention to her dress and by a graceful manner. She has, moreover, an engaging name: Madame La Charmotte. "She looked a very attractive old lady, as she sat there in her violet-coloured gown. Her neck was encircled with a frill of lace. Her arms, still beautiful, were bare, save for a flowing shawl of lace which came down to her elbows. Her powdered hair was combed back from her brow into a beautiful snow-white wave framed in a lovely bonnet of tulle. On her cheeks she had put a touch of rouge, the effect of which reminded one of an eighteenth-century pastel. A few rings glittered on her firm and tapering fingers. From time to time she tapped the ground impatiently with the high heel of her little shoe. This was of black kid, with a large buckle of marcasite which stood out against the mauve embroidered stocking. A handkerchief, scented with her favourite perfume, displayed its embroideries upon the table, and by its side was a pair of large tortoise-shell spectacles which Mme La Charmotte wore only occasionally, because 'it looked well'. Her eyesight was still in excellent condition."

It must be admitted that this old lady was privileged. A pleasant old age such as Mme de Maintenon had in mind is not exactly common. This is what constitutes the charm of Mme La Charmotte and others like her. . . .

* * *

They make a point of being fond of youth, even though they themselves have said good-bye to it. And that is all to the good. We remember that the sages of antiquity also recommended old men to associate with the young, to be present at their games, and even to take part in them if they could do so without making themselves ridiculous. . . . But for them this youthful entourage was not much more than a decorative background, an entertainment for the eye and the imagination. In reality, contact between youth and age is practically impossible. They do not understand each other. Their tastes are not the same; neither are their pleasures. To tell the whole of the unpleasant truth, they have an obscure feeling of being enemies . . . rivals . . . right up to the very brink of the grave. Racine had no love for old Corneille, and it is highly probable that this antagonism, this secret jealousy, was mutual. Old cats cuff their young ones pretty sharply. For affection to be possible between the old and the young there must be kinship, the tender interest of a father, or a grandfather. Another bond is that of religion, the intimacy of master and disciple. A spiritual director can form close relations with a catechumen or a penitent, a professor of philosophy with a favourite pupil. So much the better if the master or director is also young. Père Clérissac, the young Dominican, had certainly more influence over Ernest Psichari [1] than the Catos of his order would have had.

This affection of progenitors for their progeny often meets with no response. As the father of a very spoilt child used sadly to say to me: "Affection goes down from father to son, but it does not come up again." An old man sees little return for the love he lavishes on the young; at the same time we must

[1] Grandson of Renan and friend of Maritain and Péguy. Killed in action, 22 Aug., 1914.

remember that the reserve of love in the human heart is strictly limited. Another of my acquaintances made this remark: "To love one's children is only right and proper, but as for grandchildren, well, I must confess that mine don't interest me overmuch!"

There can be little doubt about it. It is no easy problem to find a bond of union between the two extreme periods of life.

* * *

What is the object of having the illusion of youth through association with young people, when we are not only convinced of our superiority but are conscious of having entered on a time of life that has no cause for envying those which have preceded it?

It is a sign of vanity common to every age to believe that one's own time is followed by nothing but decadence and decay. Those in their 'teens who despise their elders are despised in their turn by their juniors. I remember, when I first entered the University, the Rector, evidently rather ill at ease about the extreme youthfulness of my appearance, asked me my age. I replied, with mingled embarrassment and humility: "I'm afraid I'm very old, Sir. I'm twenty-two!"

In the army it is commonly supposed that no one is of any use after he has passed the age of sixty. "We want young generals like Bonaparte!" This may well be so, and yet the old ones are retained as long as possible, and in responsible positions, where powers of physical endurance are not required, but where mental qualities are all-important.

The fact is that the sixtieth year marks the commencement of a new career. This may last for a considerable time, even until the advent of complete decrepitude, which, however, may never come to pass. There have been nonagenarians who have died in full possession of their intellectual faculties, and even their physical energy has been sufficient for their new mode of life. I was present at a lecture, lasting an hour and a half, given by Cardinal de Cabrières when he was ninety-two years old. He stood all the time, spoke without notes, and never lost his hold upon his audience (which cannot be said of every lecturer).

I have a friend, seventy years of age, a man of ardent faith—looked on as a visionary by some of those who know him—who is a dreamer of a dangerous kind, and yet a realist; in fact, in some respects, no pair of feet could be more firmly planted on the ground than his. Starting from nothing, he has built up a considerable fortune. He has founded a host of enterprises that more than pay their way; he has cleared and colonized whole tracts of land. He might well rest content with what he has accomplished, but not a bit of it! That was only the first stage for him; he is still looking ahead. The period of high hopes, of vast ideas, has only just arrived for him. Having founded industrial establishments, he is now playing with the thought of creating universities, of building churches, of civilizing continents. This ex-professor of history—for the man of action began his career as a pedagogue, as a wielder of the pen—quotes me the case of Cardinal Ximenes, or Cardinal Fleury, who were over seventy when they began their careers as statesmen. The essential requisites, he tells me, is to have faith and to enjoy good health. Accordingly, this septuagenarian keeps himself well by careful living, and similarly, the man of business begins and ends his day with a reading from St. Paul —for him the classical example of the apostle and man of action—and half an hour's meditation. Though constantly engaged in the most terrestrial occupations, he lives in a continual exaltation of the spirit. . . .

Similarly, missionaries and heads of religious orders derive incredible energy and activity from their apostolic zeal. Some authorities aver that in war one is never beaten unless one wants to be. Can it be the same with old age? Are we old only when we agree to age?

Most politicians put up a splendid fight against old age. In some cases it would seem that their stamina is increased tenfold together with their lucidity of mind. Clemenceau, for instance, and Jules Cambon, to say nothing of Talleyrand. Are politics a specifically suitable employment for old age? Does the practical mind need to be decanted, to rid itself, with the passage of the years, of an excess of richness, and adventurous exuberance? However that may be, we observe that aged politicians cling to politics as if their very life depended on them. With death in their soul they bid farewell to power and honours. But it is never a last fare-well. At the first opportunity that offers they are ready for the fray again. . . .

* * *

Those who have been deprived of power have, like Thiers, the consolation of their " beloved studies."

Can one really work to the very end? Is great intellectual activity permitted to the old? There are any number of illustrious examples. With good health and eyesight, anyone may work, that is to say, keep himself informed of what the world is doing, verify, read, write, and judge. And create? Can one create, after a certain age? Here, too, there is no lack of affirmative examples. One might easily maintain that the finest verses written by Victor Hugo and Lamartine—the most profound, the most condensed, the most pure in tone—were their last. But we must not be led astray by exceptional examples, such as the *Œdipus Coloneus*. There is no doubt but that the fire, the power, the brilliance, of the imagination decrease with age. But even suppos-ing that all these faculties remain intact, we no longer have the same confidence in ourselves. We no longer apply ourselves to our work with the same faith, the same love. We have seen too much. Satiety is coming over us. The world loses colour, the representation of life no longer has the same interest, for we are losing interest in life itself.

In the speculative order a similar change takes

place. The time for great scientific discoveries, for great metaphysical adventures, is passed. We cease inventing systems; we even harbour a growing distrust of them. But a sense of reality, critical acumen, historical insight, the faculty of judgement, are preserved and even developed. In the intellectual field, then, the aged are still capable of rendering valuable service to their fellow-mortals.

* * *

And now, what of the pleasures of this period of life? What pleasures is it permitted to enjoy?

In this matter we have no such clearly defined rules as had the ancients. We have no method wherewith to resist senility, to preserve the memory, the youthfulness of the mind, the will to remain young —or even our physical strength. Similarly, we pay but little attention to the regulation of our pleasures. We adjust our mode of living to the inspiration of the moment or the requirements of the senses.

Abstinence and moderation ought to be the rule, and the rule ought to be adapted to the individual temperament and character. Sooner or later there comes a time when we must make up our mind not to go to this or that place, not to eat this, or drink that, not to dine in Town, not to go to the theatre. M. de Fontanes, the first Grand Master of the Université de France, used to say that his ideal of pleasure was "a good dinner followed by a good, and really indecent, ballet." Apoplexy accounted for M. de Fontanes. The pleasures of the table, and even the mere pleasures of the eyes, may be fatal for old men. A draught of cold air on the steps of a casino may mean death to an elderly, incautious lady who has not been able to break herself of the habit of frequenting fashionable resorts and of retiring late to bed. Antique wisdom, on the other hand, had it that it was best to make an early start with being old if one wanted to be old for long, unless, of course, one preferred that dangerous maxim, "short and sweet." But we all know to what that leads.

Not to go abroad too much, not to show oneself too much: that would seem to be a good rule of health and conduct for the old. Over-anxiety to mingle with the young is also to be avoided. An aged face depresses them; it brings before their eyes a *memento mori*. It reminds them of the grave. Even the sight of an illustrious old man somehow displeases them, unless it is masked in glory; and it is not the oldness that they admire in a glorious old man; it is the immortal laurels.

* * *

Finally, unlike the ancients, we have no notion how to prepare ourselves for the great departure. We certainly do not consider "life as a meditation on death." In this respect, even Catholicism seems to have greatly relaxed its precepts, or rather the rule has bowed to the frivolity of modern times. In the seventeenth century Christian deaths, in the strict sense of the word, were frequent. A great number of them were extraordinarily heroic or edifying, notably those of men and women who had scandalized their contemporaries: the Princess Palatine—to mention only the most famous—the Duchess de La Vallière, Mme de Montespan, and Mme de Monaco, "whose face," when she died, "was no longer human"—or even those of criminals, such as the Marquise de Brinvilliers and La Voisin. . . . They had no fear of death. They waited for it steadfastly, made lengthy preparations for it, and looked it in the face when it eventually arrived. Consider the instance of the statesman Pontchartrain. Believing his hour to be at hand, he resigned his office as Secretary of State, and disregarding the remonstrances of the king and of his associates, shut himself up in the Oratory, where, for years on end, he did nothing but meditate on death. . . .

* * *

But, once again, all this takes for granted a period of peace, a spacious and secure life, or at least the leisure and tranquillity that go with an adequate income. We have confined our attention almost exclusively to those "blessed with this world's goods." What a consolation to offer to the herd of wretches for whom existence is nothing but suffering and hardship from the cradle to the grave—to the countless thousands for whom old age is the worst calamity of all?

Yet both these classes are united in one common plight : their equal liability to suffer pain.

CHAPTER VI

ACCEPTANCE

ONE of my *confrères*, who is a novelist, an historian, and a man of imagination and intense interior life, writes to me as follows:

"I am over sixty, and you would like to know how I am feeling. I will tell you.

"Physically, I am well enough, though my congenital defects are making themselves felt more and more as time goes on. I think I know the disease, or diseases, to which I shall eventually succumb; I am already a prey to them from time to time. Nevertheless, my health is better than it has ever been before. Mentally, I think I can lay claim, if not exactly to an improvement in my faculties, at least to an increasing clarity of mind and, conjointly, to a feeling of deliverance, to a serenity, a peace, that I have never before experienced.

"I appreciate this all the more for having had a painful, anxious, and tormented youth, with no feeling of security but with a continual fear for the future, the continual worry of overwhelming responsibilities. You may wonder how I managed to survive. There must be various states of grace, and the most beneficial of them is complete oblivion. If I had had a clear idea of all the calamities that were weighing on my mind I should probably have broken down.

"Physical calamities are the least important. Except for an attack of arthritis that lasted for nearly a year, I have been free from serious illness, but in my childhood and my early youth I was continually subject to indisposition and petty illnesses, and all the time I was a prey to nervous irritation. I was born tired and ailing, over-sensitive, and easily upset. This went on for years, and I suffered acutely from my nerves, which were set on edge still more by the strain on my system when I began to grow, by privation, by insufficient nourishment, by an unhealthy mode of life. In addition to these physical disadvantages I was mentally depressed. My imagination probably caused me more suffering than my body. For several winters, misled by superficial symptoms, I thought I was consumptive. Every year when the leaves began to fall I said good-bye to life. And then, in the course of time, my living conditions improved and with them my health. At the present time, having passed my sixtieth year, I cannot exactly say that I am hale and hearty —it is clear that my strength and activity have appreciably diminished—but my vital tone has become much more stabilized. And I suffer far less than I used to do. It may be that I have become accustomed to it. Whatever the reason, the fact remains that pain has less effect on me now; it seems to have grown weaker and its visitations are fewer and farther between. The result is that I can truthfully say that old age has presented me with a sort—an imperfect sort, of course—of physical well-being.

"Like most of us, I still have worries about the future, whatever little future still remains for me to look forward to. This is excusable, I think, considering the present unsettled state of things. None of us can see a day ahead. But in spite of this, my anxieties are not as acutely tragic as they used to be. I am more confident about my means of existence, and consequently I attach less importance to material considerations. I am more detached from all those things that formerly were indispensable to me. A sort of indifference has crept over me with regard to my lot in this world. I am prepared for anything.

"As far as I personally am concerned, the most precious benefit I owe to old age is freedom from passion.

"How glorious to feel oneself emancipated, permanently exempt from service! What a dream of delight, what an unimaginably delicious rest! I still feel the spur of nature now and then—that never dies away completely, even if it comes only by way of the memory, in fits and starts—but the imagination refuses henceforward to throw a halo round the passionate or voluptuous mirage; and when the desired object loses its halo, pleasure loses its fascination. It appears in all its nakedness, in all its wretchedness, as a miserable physiological phenomenon. The worn-out bull refuses to allow itself to be infuriated by the red tinsel of the bandillero.

Someone has called it 'love without wings'. To ensure our peace of mind let us old men build temples and altars, let us pour out libations, in honour of the frigid deity, Eros Apteros. . . . With the young Alfred de Musset we are now mature enough to expostulate:

> Love, master of the world, execrable folly,
> Bound to pleasure by such a fragile bond!

"We know only too well that love—that is passionate love, or promiscuous love—is not by any means all pleasure. For a long time now I have been convinced that not only is it the most unreasonable of stupidities, but the most thankless business, that which pays the least, that in which we are 'stung' most badly. It appears that there is always a certain number of 'old campaigners'. Well, I have retired for good. What joy, when the campaign has been such a gruelling one!

"We have only to remember how much we suffer when we are in that ridiculous and pitiful condition, how much we endure for such a meagre, illusory result. To think of the humiliation, the distasteful relations (in promiscuous love), the despicable actions, the worries of every description, not excluding money-troubles—and they are not the least— and lastly the revulsion of feeling that is the price of these fleeting pleasures! The torment of having to pursue a creature who does not love you, who can never love you, or—to put things in their most favourable light—who will never love you as you want to be loved. Even in a case of perfect reciprocity—which is most unlikely—how distressing it is suddenly to feel that a passion that would like to be eternal is only ephemeral and is compelled to act a lie in its frantic efforts to prolong its life! And yet we have to experience all this, otherwise we should think that we had been deprived of the only good in life. What a painful swindle the whole thing is!

"Some people say: 'Noble passions and ideals are all nonsense. Sentimentality in sex affairs is a deplorable stupidity.' Take rather as your guiding principle the saying of M. de Buffon: 'The only good things in life are physical.' . . . This view is shared to some extent by prostitutes. In a recent work by François Mauriac, a professional lady tells us that 'that is the only thing to be said in its favour, the only thing that doesn't let you down'. This, then, is why so many old men are sexual addicts—to say nothing of their desire to emulate their juniors—this is why they give way to a folly that is as grotesque as it is pernicious.

"I have never forgotten a shocking accident that happened to one of my old school-friends. He had kept himself pure till he was twenty, and then one fine day he allowed himself to be taken home by a woman of the streets. As a result of this one act of debauchery—and his first act—he forfeited the ability ever to repeat it. The illness he contracted from this vulgar dissipation soon became tubercular. The disease had to be pulled out by the roots, so to speak—so radically indeed that the poor young fellow found himself reduced to impotence. He was desperately upset about the matter, and I made every possible effort to console him, but without effect. Assuming an air of conviction, I used to say to him: 'Don't worry. You're not missing much. It's a greatly overrated pleasure!' But I didn't believe a word of what I said. It was not till long afterwards that I realized that I had been speaking words of wisdom.

" 'It's the only good thing there is!' So the saying goes, but it's not a true one—unless, of course, one's demands are very humble. Flaubert speaks of vertiginous heights of sensuality, of endless spirals of voluptuousness that give rise to further voluptuousness. Possibly he is right, but the greater part of these pleasures is due to the imagination. 'They are the pleasures of the brain', said Maupassant, who knew his subject well. It is very rarely that both parties want the same thing simultaneously. When one of them wants to give, the other is not in a receptive mood. When one is passionate, the other is like a block of wood. But even supposing everything has gone off well; the two parties congratulate themselves and thank each other, but one of them is nearly always cheated.

"No, I have no regrets for what has gone. If I answer the call of instinct I do so without glorying in it; on the contrary, I take it as a humiliation, as an act of constraint on the part of Nature, from whose attentions the sooner we are completely freed the better. And, thank Heavens, the bonds that bind us to it will break of their own accord. Let us bury our youthful folly with a light heart and erect a triple cross above its grave!

"As for passionate love, it has receded so far into the past that the very idea of it is strange to me. But I am still capable of sharing a calm, reposeful affection: conjugal affection, the affection that remains when desire has been appeased—provided that there is no disturbing residue of passion—and finally the pure joys of friendship. This is what I mean by liberation. We give without enslaving ourselves. We give gratuitously. We ask nothing in return. We take what comes our way, with no illusions but with peace of mind. . . . Blessed be old age, which metes us out these joys!

"In the intellectual sphere the blessings of old age are even greater. I have never had such mental pleasure, I have never felt my intellect to be so wide-awake—I am referring to the intellect pure and simple, as distinct from the imagination, the gift of eloquence, or anything connected with talents of a physical nature.

"In my capacity of novelist I was under the impression for many years that the highest mental faculty was what we are pleased to call the gift of creation. To evolve a plot, to fill in the background, to delineate the characters, to follow their career through all the vicissitudes of an artificial destiny—that, to my mind, was the highest expression of the inventive faculty. I am not so dazzled by it nowadays. Invention, properly so called, may play but a minor part, if any part at all, in the mimicry which consists largely of technique and acquired virtuosity. It is a rather stupid game, which only a genius can make worth while—a game which nearly everybody thinks himself capable of playing. Total strangers write to me by every post to tell me what wonderful stories their lives would make, and they invariably proceed to relate them themselves. Even unusual stories have no interest for me unless they reveal some hidden recesses of the human soul or throw fresh light on some fundamental thought. And even in the latter case I often wonder whether this thought, or psychological truth, would not be better expressed, discussed, and placed in its proper setting by some other method than those of the novelist or dramatist. I am interested, not so much in the brilliance of an idea as in its accuracy. Life is too short for me now to chase after anything but truth.

"Possibly another reason why I am not so dazzled by the art of mimicry as I used to be is that having to practise it professionally has made it too easy for me; also, and most decidedly, because I have lost my youthful enthusiasm for life and the art that reproduces it; because the freshness of the world, the virginity of emotion, have gone from me for ever. This loss has been replaced by distrust, by an increasingly keener realization of the artificiality of literature and æsthetics. Thanks to this distrust, to this distaste for artificiality, I have been freed from my adolescent snobbishness, from my ridiculous enthusiasm, from the naivety of the stripling who has as yet seen nothing of life, knows nothing about it, and thinks to find it in the imaginary world of literature. I am on my guard against unknown geniuses and nine days' wonders foisted on us by the Press. I do not believe that talent is synonymous

G 2

with youth. On the contrary, I confess that the longer I live the further removed I am from youth. There seems to be a wall between us that increases in height and thickness. It is all my fault, I know, because I make no effort to establish relations with them. I tell myself that I haven't the time, that I have other things to do, things that are more important, more pressing. Some of my friends who are even senior to me have warned me that unless I mend my ways I am likely to drift into a senile incapacity for appreciation. I am reminded of Sainte-Beuve and Taine, who failed to understand Baudelaire, for want of fellow-feeling. There is no doubt that they failed to understand him, but their old age had nothing to do with the matter. Sainte-Beuve failed because he was riddled with the jealousy and the pettiness of an unsuccessful poet—Taine, because Baudelaire upset his theories of the beneficence of art and shocked his donnish prudery.

"My contention is that old age, while strengthening our judgement, purifies our taste and refines our feelings. We become immune to the dust thrown in our eyes; we become less liable to be taken in by booby-traps.

"To judge and appreciate, calmly, dispassionately —that is the privilege of old age. A feeling for truth and reality becomes more and more predominant. Hence my increasing preference for history—because it is truer than fiction. At least that is the reason, or pretext, with which I persuade myself. You may think, perhaps, that the study of man made 'from the life'—the function of the novelist—is less likely to err than that made from a distance and with the aid of documents that are always suspect. Well, it may be that my contemporaries either do not interest me or that they irritate me with ideas and fashions that I have discarded, whereas the past provides me with a new field of observation in which there is nothing to offend me, or if there is something that offends me or arouses my indignation it is tempered by the pleasure that I take in understanding it. But I think that even the psychology of people that are dead and gone—and who, at bottom, are strangely similar to the present population of the world—is beginning to pall on me. It seems that the only thing that interests me nowadays is to understand the law that governs events, to view the present in the womb of the past, to watch the chaos of the past straighten itself out and explain itself by the light of an idea or central fact. This is probably the source of the greatest intellectual enjoyment, and this is doubtless why history is so attractive for an old man like myself.

"I fully realize that many of my faculties are weakening, my memory in particular. Alas, unlike the ancients, I do not take the trouble to exercise it, to keep it in good trim, like the Pythagoreans. My pockets are full of notes and memoranda. My tottering memory has to go about on crutches. But what does that matter when my mind has become an instrument of precision, extremely sensitive, extremely delicate, extremely accurate? This feeling of mastery compensates me for all my losses.

"There is just one thing that worries me from time

to time in the obscure reaches of my soul—an instinctive worry that I ought to conquer with the least possible delay—I mean the distressing thought that time is slipping through my hands. Every night, on retiring, I say to myself: 'Another day nearer the end!' How different from the past, when I felt that I had an inexhaustible number of days to waste! I remember my feeling of resilience on recovering from the only serious illness I have ever had, when I was nearly thirty. What an intoxicating feeling of rebirth! What a fearless rush towards the future! . . . At forty came the first attack, the first cry of alarm in the regions of the subconscious. At fifty: gloom, mitigated by the hope of a leisurely advance to sixty, of husbanding my resources, of putting a stop to the reckless prodigality of yore. And the sixtieth year arrives at breakneck speed. We give in, but there is always a tightening of the heart-strings as every evening we register the death of another day, as we note the dwindling of our treasure. We frantically exhort ourselves not to lose a minute. And then the distress calms down at the thought that if this existence were to last for ever, life would be more horrible than death. . . .

"Such is my condition; and taken all in all, there is nothing tragical about it. It is not only endurable, but in many ways positively pleasant. Nevertheless, I must admit that what makes it tolerable is the knowledge that my means of existence are assured, together with the ever-present possibility of work and pleasure, and the absence, not only of serious worries but, above all, of serious pain. But who can tell what tomorrow has in store? Under the present régime of spoliation and an equally low standard of living for all, one has to be prepared to be reduced to beggary at a moment's notice. Social improvements are not being made on our behalf. We shall have to work until we drop—that is if we are allowed to work at all. . . . But even supposing that these misfortunes never come to pass, how shall I fare when I make the acquaintance of physical pain enhanced by mental suffering, both at their maximum intensity? How am I to deal with desperate, intolerable pain, prolonged for endless days and nights?"

* * *

This intimate confession brings me back once more to the same obsessing thought: old age would be nothing if it were exempt from pain. Who would not be willing to grow old, if he were certain of not suffering?

Suffering! Must we all pass through that narrow gate? If so, how are we to bear it?

PART II

SUFFERING

"Shall we force the general law of nature, which in every living creature under heaven, is seen to tremble under pain?"

MONTAIGNE
Essays, XL. (tr. by Charles Cotton).

CHAPTER I

A MORNING AT THE SALPÊTRIÈRE

O N a beautiful morning in November, 1925, a frosty, sunny morning, Paul Bourget, Dr. Charles Fiessinger, and I met outside the iron gates of the Salpêtrière, at the junction of the three streets converging on the entrance and the two wings of the façade.

The clock in the dome had only just struck nine. What had brought us to this old Parisian hospice, with its rather sinister name, at such an early hour? The doctor was at home there, or at any rate he was in a world with which he was familiar. Nor was it surprising that the writer famed for his psychological insight, who took such a keen interest in every medical discovery and theory, should be standing at the entrance to the sanctuary of modern psychiatry. My presence there, beside the two doctors, was rather more remarkable. What did I want at the Salpêtrèire, I, who have always had a holy dread of hospitals, of clinics, of human rubbish-heaps, of every place where there is suffering and death? Only a question of the highest literary and scientific importance could have forced me to conquer my repugnance.

I was engaged at the time in studying the mystical life of St. Teresa of Avila. The morbid phenomena that either accompanied, preceded, or followed her ecstasies certainly came within the sphere of medicine, but was medicine entitled to take possession of the ecstasies themselves? Was it qualified to deal with them? A whole library of literature answered me proudly in the affirmative. With an admirable intrepidity it assured me that cases equivalent or analogous to that of St. Teresa were to be found in any hospital or padded cell. In such places apparitions, the sensing of an invisible presence, stigmata, levitations—all these extra-ordinary manifestations, were everyday affairs, and not only there, but even in the ordinary walks of life, among every class of society throughout the world. This is the kind of letter that used to be addressed to me: "We have a patient here who says she plays word games with the three Persons of the Holy Trinity." . . . And the fine-sounding word 'hysterics', which since Charcot's time was accepted as an explanation for everything, was hastily pro-nounced as a final conclusion and an indisputable diagnosis. . . .

Were such identifications permissible? Did the analogies which had been cited actually exist? If they did, where could I make more complete and reliable observations than in the Salpêtrière, where for centuries past every variety of nervous malady had received attention and on which Charcot's teaching had bestowed a scientific prestige that showed no sign of waning? And what better guides and introducers could I have had? One of them, who might well have been known as 'Doctor'

Bourget, was the writer of psychological fiction who had no hesitation in appealing to medicine to explain certain phenomena of passion and sentiment and has thus transformed the methods of his art. The other, my old friend Charles Fiessinger, possessed one of the most supple and unprejudiced minds that one could meet with in his profession, always on his guard against the exaggerations and blunders that lie in wait for the doctrinaire—in other words, he was a man with a sufficiently lively sense of realities to recognize the limits of scientific knowledge and the special domain of religion and mysticism.

* * *

I acknowledge straightway that the mere look of the place on that sunny winter morning put me in a favourable frame of mind: the gardens, genuinely French, the imposing façade, the dome of the church of St. Louis that overlooks the magnificent array of buildings, the pavilions constructed by Levau, the arms of Mazarin sculptured in the tympanum of one of the attics, in short, the regal aspect of that Suffering City, a town within a town. . . . I confess that all this lessened my repugnance to an extraordinary degree. And when I say that we were received in the most cordial and flattering manner by Professor Guillain, the head of the medical staff of the Salpêtrière, and by his colleagues and students, it will be understood that my disappointment at not finding there what I was looking for was all the keener.

93

The very first words I had with these eminent practitioners robbed me of every one of my illusions. I was told not only that the major part of Charcot's theories had been abandoned—although, it was admitted, he had opened up a most productive avenue of research—but that the 'subjects' who had formed the material for his work were no longer in existence, or, at any rate, were becoming rarer every day. They had no more cases of hysteria, nor, for the moment, of religious mania. The *soi-disant* instances of levitation had never been scientifically confirmed. As for stigmatics, all they had to show me was a poor girl with a supersensitive skin, on which the mark of a cross traced with the finger or the wrong end of a pencil would remain visible for some little time. But this had nothing whatever to do with the subjects of obvious miracles on which the stigmata appeared of their own accord, so to speak; still less had it anything to do with St. Teresa. And when I asked for a scientific definition of hysteria, I was told that hysterics were extinct; there were only nervous ailments with extremely complex symptoms to which no precise definition could be applied and which were very difficult to bring within any common principle.

This visit, then, interesting though it was, brought me no nearer the object of my search. The Salpêtrière was not, as I had been told, the great infirmary for mystics. There was nothing there that, 'scientifically' speaking, could explain, or throw any light on, the ecstasies of St. Teresa. But the remarks let fall by the master and his pupils on the subject of their studies compensated me to a large extent for my initial disappointment. Furthermore, under the influence of the highly abnormal atmosphere and the deeply moving sights that passed before my eyes, I suddenly became aware of certain ideas and feelings that hitherto had been withheld from me. In effect, my visit to the Salpêtrière, like the one I paid, later on, to Bicêtre, under the guidance of another eminent practitioner, Dr. Alajouanine, left a profound impression on my mind.

* * *

The sights I saw were not exactly shocking; there was nothing that might be described as a grand spectacle of suffering. Hospital wards are generally peaceful; one suffers there in silence. But specimens of physical wreckage, of moral degradation, were there in plentiful variety; and without inspecting any of them individually, I became acquainted with the population of incurables and insane that inhabit the Salpêtrière. I felt literally oppressed, physically embarrassed, by all that suffering around me, that mass of degeneration, torture, and agony, that long array of victims ranged beneath the rough-hewn beams and along the untreated walls of the wards, like a symbol and permanent exhibition of the suffering world: it was the oppression I had always experienced on entering a hospital, clinic, or infirmary. By an irony of fate, I, who have an instinctive horror of these places, was condemned throughout my youth to frequent them, to witness sufferings and death-agonies, the mere sight of which killed all my joy in life. Visiting the sick and dying has been my lot for many a year, but that morning of November, 1925, was the first time I had crossed the threshold of a hospital for a considerable period. My repugnance and my depression came back to me with renewed force, together with a sort of shame in being free and in feeling well in that prison and torture-chamber.

I was also struck by the contrast between the misery that surrounded me and the royal pomp displayed in certain portions of the building. The Salpêtrière, as seen from the river-side, has the aspect of a palace; and when one draws near to it one is surprised by the beauty and grandeur of its architecture. This magnificent congeries of buildings, emblazoned with the crown and the arms of France, and with the sheaves and the hat of the cardinalate, was originally destined as an asylum for beggars, ne'er-do-wells, vicious children, cutpurses, prostitutes, idiots, epileptics, and other human off-scourings of a large city. Whence this antithesis between the pomp of the edifice and the sad realities concealed therein? Nowadays, our hospitals have no such stylish grandeur; they are dully utilitarian, strictly adapted to the needs of their guests and the demands of modern hygiene. They are merely infirmaries and laboratories, frequently nothing more than human stables. Those of olden days, such as the Salpêtrière, Bicêtre, the Invalides, the hospices in the large provincial towns, even in an unassuming town like Beaune,

have a symbolic significance far surpassing their
external object.

In erecting these imposing buildings their
founders did not intend them to serve as refuges
for the under-dogs of society, nor as jails for foot-
pads, but for the reception of "the living members
of Jesus Christ." Well, Christ is King; therefore He
must have a royal reception. A hospice is not a
philanthropic or prophylactic work resulting from
hypocrisy or fear. It is a work of love and a token
of adoration. The charter authorizing the foundation of the Salpêtrière expresses these lofty motives
in unmistakable terms: "regarding," said the Royal
Chancellor, "the unfortunate poor as the living
members of Jesus Christ, not as useless members of
the State, and participating in the execution of this
great work, not for the purpose of maintaining
public order, but moved by purely charitable
motives. . . ."

This, then, was the governing idea that brought
about the erection of this hospital. This palace was
not constructed because of fear or repulsion, nor for
the efficient policing of the city; but to bear witness
to the charity of man for his fellow-man who has
been redeemed by Christ. Naturally enough, in
actual practice, the managers of this lofty enterprise may have lost sight of the generous thought
that originally inspired it. Evil forces Good in sheer
self-defence to treat it on its merits. But the thought
was surely this: a hospital is an act of love and
respect for human suffering. It is an affirmation of
the fact that suffering is not a chance accident of

life, a shameful disgrace to be hidden out of sight, but, like poverty, its near relation, something sacred that ought to inspire veneration. Christ, who is life, is also the Man of Suffering, and that before being the God of Glory. . . .

Transposing this idea into philosophical language, we find Schopenhauer telling us that suffering is sacred because it is a means of purification and liberation, a means of transcending life. Life is pain. Pain is congenital with life; it is the very stuff of which life is made. And thus it binds all the living into the solidarity of the same original evil. It cannot but inspire them with an immense sympathy with one another and at the same time with an immense desire for liberation or redemption. Hence the sacred character of pain; it is through pain that we enter into communion with our brethren, and it is through pain that we are able to be delivered: it is the sole means of enfranchisement—enfranchisement from the pain of living. Pain is a deity of liberation, and as such it deserves to have temples erected in its honour. Every home of human suffering ought, like the hospices of our ancestors, to have the majesty of temples. . . .

These were the thoughts I took away with me from my visit to the Salpêtrière, and later, when I decided to write on the subject of pain, the memory of this visit was revived. Though it had failed to satisfy my curiosity it had given rise to reflections that have, perhaps, formed a fitting introduction to the pages that will follow.

CHAPTER II

PAIN

THOUGH it is true that pain may come upon us at any period of our life, there can be no doubt that it is the special lot of old age. And even when, by some rare chance, old age is exempt, it is only to fall a prey to a host of infirmities that are often more irksome than grievous pain. Nevertheless, it is grievous pain that we fear the most; it is this that subjects the human organism to the roughest trial; and it is this more than anything else that is likely to drive the imagination frantic.

I am not going to treat this subject in any free and easy manner. It is a terrible thought that at any moment we may have to undergo these tortures and that only too often they can take possession of the whole of a wretched human life.

According to the doctors, the worst of all pains are those resulting from certain wounds or lesions, such as those of childbirth, but above all, those brought about by serious illnesses, such as cancer, angina pectoris, and locomotor ataxy. Though extremely violent, they are not continuous. They are followed, or interrupted, by more or less lengthy periods of remission. But even these pauses are rendered painful by the apprehension, or the certainty, that the pain will come again. In anticipation of the coming torture, the imagination of the

H 2

victim exaggerates it. Or very possibly reflection intervenes and putting the evidence before him with pitiless rigour forces him to realize the irremediable progress of the evil.

* * *

There has been published recently, under the depressing title of *La Doulou*,[1] a collection of notes taken by Alphonse Daudet when suffering from marasmus. Day by day for several years he noted the development of his illness, its crises, its sudden onslaughts. He kept his suffering under careful observation and he has expressed it with an acuteness and an intensity that make it penetrate into the very fibre of the reader's soul. He instructs us as to what suffering is, he teaches us how to suffer, and how to react against it, and how we can derive from it instruction for ourselves, even moral benefit for ourselves and for others—and this with a self-abnegation that borders at times on heroism.

He shows us how the first symptoms escape our notice. We do not become aware of them till later, when the illness has definitely declared itself. "Very old premonitory symptoms. Extraordinary pains: great spurts of flame cutting through my carcass and lighting it up. . . . Burning of the eyes. Horrible pain of reverberation. . . ." Then the symptoms engage his attention still more forcibly: "Susceptibility to noises: shovel and tongs in the fireplace. The rending effect of bells. Ticking of the watch;

[1] A familiar term for *douleur*, pain.

spider's web begun at four in the morning. . . .
Supersensitiveness of the skin, shortening of sleep,
then spitting of blood. . . ." Finally the illness is
confirmed: "The breastplate! The first sensations
I have had of it. It began with a stifling feeling. I
sat up in bed, terrified. . . . Every night contraction
of the ribs . . . frightful. . . . Like a steel belt pressing in the loins . . . with buckle-pins like glowing
coals and sharp as needles. . . . For months, ever
since I have had this breastplate round me, I have
not been able to unhook myself, to breathe. . . ."

And now he must suffer at the mere approach of
pain. "It is very strange, the fear that pain gives
me now, this pain at least. It is bearable, and yet *I
cannot bear it*. It is horrible—and the call for anæsthetics like a call for help, the screeching of a woman
in the face of real danger. . . ."

Next, pain in its most violent, cruellest form.
"What I suffered last night in my heel and my ribs!
What torture! . . . Impossible to describe it. One
would have to scream. . . . Of what use are words
for what we feel when pain—or passion—has us in its
grip? They come when everything is over, calmed
down; they speak of memories, either impotent or
lying." Nevertheless, he attempts to define the
indefinable, to express the inexpressible, to omit no
note in the whole gamut of pain. He classifies "the
forms of pain": knives thrust beneath the toe-nail,
the torture of the 'boot' round the ankles, sharp
little rats' teeth gnawing at the toes. And what he
calls the *Crociato:* "Yes, that was what it was last
night. The torture of the Cross, the twisting of the

hands, the feet, the knees, the nerves pulled out to breaking-point. And the rough cord binding my body, and the lance-thrusts in my ribs. To appease my thirst, a spoonful of iodized bromide, bitterly salt, on my parched, swollen, cracked, encrusted lips: it was the sponge dipped in vinegar and gall. . . ."

Pain seizes possession of the entire being; it reigns as absolute master. "Pain resounds in my poor carcass, hollowed out by anæmia, like a voice in a house bare of furniture or wall-covering. Days, whole days, when there was nothing living within me but suffering. . . . Everything is leaving me. . . . I am engulfed in darkness. . . . Good-bye, my wife, my children, my own ones, so dear to my heart. . . . Good-bye, myself, my dear self, so obscured, so dim. . . ."

And yet the insufferable torture still goes on: "My pain fills the horizon, fills everything. . . . I cry out like a blind man, 'Everything is dark!' This is the colour of my whole life now. . . . At present it is a bitter, stagnant, painful torpor. Indifference to everything. *Nada! . . . Nada! . . .*"

Lastly, pain destroys even thought itself—but now pain is sought for, longed for; it puts a stop to the working of the intellect, that sees too clearly, that doubles the victim's suffering by showing him the inexorable progress of the illness, the hopeless illness. "Ah! How well I understand the Russian who prefers to suffer! Only yesterday he said to me: 'Pain stops me thinking'." Further on we read: "Ah! How many times we have to die before we really do so! . . ."

Suffering makes us malevolent when it lasts as
long as this. It embitters us; it exasperates us with
everything around us. The patient becomes irrit-
able, malicious, as though, surfeited with suffering,
he would like to make others suffer, too. Worst of
all, perhaps, is to feel the intellect becoming
atrophied, sterile, refusing to obey the will, which
fumes and rages. "Sterility! The only word which
is anywhere near expressing the horrible state of
stagnation into which the intellect lapses from time
to time. It is the 'lack of faith and fervour of
believing souls'. The note that I throw out here,
inexpressive and dull, written in one of these cruel
phases, speaks only for me. . . ."

The only respite is the insensibility procured by
poisonous sedatives. "Heavenly lulling of nights of
morphia—nights without sleep . . ." or "complete
annihilation, Erebus, the murky flood, nothingness! Delicious immersion! It catches me up and
whirls me round and round. . . ." But the awaken-
ings are terrible; the pain returns with redoubled
rage. The sole effect of the palliative, which is only
temporary, is to clear the brain and thus increase
the patient's consciousness of his ghastly plight. . . .

And then, little by little, he becomes accustomed
to it. There takes place a kind of adaptation: the
imperceptible transition from the *carcere duro* to the
carcere durissimo. The feelings of terror and despair
that belong to the first stage, die down. "Body and
mind accommodate themselves to their sinister condition." He forces himself to make his suffering his
life. "O my pain, be all in all to me! Let my eyes

find in thee the regions you take away from me! Be my philosophy, my science! . . ." This resignation develops into kindness, into a desire to be good and tender-hearted. "Pride in not imposing on others the ill-humour and the gloomy sense of injustice arising from my suffering. . . ."

There is no need, I think, to comment on this harrowing confession. It is enough to listen to these cries of anguish, to feel the pathos and the grandeur of the ultimate acceptance.

* * *

Horrible to relate, the unfortunate author had to endure this fearful illness for many years. The first attacks began in 1884, and he did not die till 1897. There was ample time, then, for the tragic adaptation he speaks of. During the periods, always precarious, when he was not in actual pain, he was able to resume his work and produce some splendid compositions. There are other diseases, perhaps, that are even worse, in that they permit of no hope whatever. They are more brutal, more rapid, but the pain is practically continuous. It is not merely that the victim is tortured corporally, his human dignity is assaulted, his body is degraded, all his distastes and delicate feelings are attacked. It is death before its time; still living, he is forced to be present at the decomposition of his corpse. He is invaded by ordure and putridity. Even while in the throes of pain he is plunged and suffocated in indescribably disgusting filth.

In this respect the last illness of Philip II was particularly horrible. For several years he had been ravaged by acute arthritis, followed by incipient dropsy: swelling of the abdomen and the extremities, painful sensitiveness of the whole body, festering sores on the fingers and toes; but during the last six weeks of his life it seemed that every conceivable form of suffering was meted out to him.

He went to die at the Escorial, the house of piety and knowledge he had himself established, among the monks whose austere rule he would have liked to follow in its entirety. No sooner had he arrived there than he had a tumour on his thigh. It was operated on, and before the scar had healed, two fistulas appeared beside the tumour. "They suppurated copiously. All this had to be dressed, which was an intolerable torture. And the large tumour, which refused to close, was continuously discharging matter; it filled two basins every day. 'The mere thought of it makes one shudder', was the comment of the monks, who viewed the sight with feelings of compassion mingled with horror and disgust. . . . But worse was yet to come. . . . Exhausted by the fever and the unceasing suppuration of the tumour and the fistulas, his limbs stiff and sore with gout, the poor sufferer could neither change his position nor even make the slightest movement. He uttered piercing shrieks if anyone so much as touched him. As a result of lying still, his shoulders and every part of his body in contact with the sheets erupted into sores. It was impossible to change his linen or to raise him up so that he could relieve his bowels; a hole had to be cut in the bed. The situation was rendered even more appalling by the fact that a medicine that he had taken had brought on an uncontrollable attack of diarrhœa, which was not to cease until he had expired. This, together with the incessant suppuration of his sores, turned his bed into a veritable dung-heap, the stench of which was insupportable.

"The poor man's ordure gradually became his winding-sheet. This was the worst agony of all for one who had been so careful in his personal hygiene, so orderly in everything, who could not bear to see a cobweb on the wall or a speck of dirt on the floor, the king who had taught cleanliness to the Spaniards, and even imposed it on them.

"All attempts to drag him out of this cesspool were in vain. One day when they raised one of his legs to dress it and clean it as far as possible, he cried out in an agony of pain: 'Stop, or I shall die!' The cry was so unnerving that they dared not continue, and were forced to leave him in his infamous condition. The sores on his shoulders and loins increased in size, and their foulness hastened on their putrefaction. The whole surface of his body gradually became one mass of infection and corruption. . . . Agonizing headaches, perpetual insomnia, and a burning thirst that nothing could assuage.

"Worst of all was the abominable stench that turned the stoutest stomach and put to flight not only the attendants but even the physicians. . . .

"In the midst of all these horrors there was one

admirable feature: the mastery over mind and soul retained by the tortured man until the very end. 'The only parts of him that were sound', wrote the annalist Sepulveda, 'were his eyes, his tongue, and his mind'. This was true, for he saw everything, heard everything, and understood everything, and all the time he spoke as a master, as one given to command. In that frightful liquefaction of the flesh, that flood of filth in which he was submerged, that paroxysm of pain, and that smell of the charnel-house, his dominating intelligence continued to impose itself on those around him. With his body subjected to the utmost depths of degradation, he was still the king. It was always possible to address him as 'Your Majesty'. This majesty, which he possessed to an eminent degree, remained intact. Even in the state to which he was reduced, this preposterous state where grotesqueness vied with ignominy, this royal majesty continued to inspire respect and even fear. Philip was formidable to the end; even the Nuncio, who came to visit him, and the Archbishop of Toledo, who gave him Extreme Unction, were overawed. . . ." [1]

* * *

To counteract his sufferings, the Catholic King, as was to be expected, relied principally on spiritual remedies. While they were operating on the tumour on his thigh he had read to him the Passion according to St. Matthew; and unto the end he comforted

[1] The foregoing passage is taken from my book, *Philippe II à l'Escorial* (L'Artisan du Livre, Paris), pp. 238 *seqq*.

himself with exhortations, pious readings, meditations, and reliquaries brought from the church and arranged on an altar of repose before his death-bed.

Our modern knowledge of antidotes to pain is almost entirely restricted to those of a material order: anæsthetics and narcotics. We boast of having conquered pain. Certainly it is a considerable feat, a great benefaction, to have rendered us insensible to the paroxysms of suffering caused by illness and operations. To say nothing of the former, the latter, when one considers the surgical methods practised by our forebears, must have been appalling. St. Augustine, in describing an operation on a fistula performed by a noted surgeon of Carthage, assures us that the patient's suffering reached the very limit of human endurance. Those who are as old as I am have only to remember the simple extraction of a molar in the days when dentists did not use even local anæsthetics. We ought to be thankful, then, to those who have saved us from so much needless suffering, but we must not take too literally the current saying that medicine has gained a decisive victory over pain, for it is true only within narrowly restricted limits. The effect of sedatives and narcotics is only temporary, and, especially in surgical operations, they are fraught with danger, to the organism which they poison. Moreover, the body adapts itself to them, the effect diminishes, the doses have to be increased, and the final result is the fatal poisoning of the system. Alphonse Daudet had frequent and almost regular recourse to bromide, chloral, morphia, and ether, but, as we have seen, they gave him neither sleep nor respite from his pain. Consequently, in spite of all the anodynes, all the highly perfected medicaments, all the care, all the treatments, his last years were one long suffering.

* * *

The ancients, who had no knowledge of either sedatives or anæsthetics, relied principally on spiritual remedies for pain, and in this respect they were clearly superior to us.

Their philosophers—like, in later days, the Christians—taught men how to suffer, just as they taught them how to grow old and how to die. For various reasons, political and social no less than material, they certainly suffered more than we do. Nowadays, human lives are less endangered, less threatened, than they have been for many thousands of years— but only in the areas that have come under the influence of Western civilization. Even now, nine-tenths of our planet are exposed to all the atrocities and all the scourges against which it has taken us so long to find an adequate protection. It is always well to remind the civilized that their civilization is fragile, limited, and superficial, and that it is barbarism that has won the day.

The protection of human life provided by ancient civilizations was sadly incomplete. One always had to be prepared to suffer, not only every sort of natural scourge, but the cruellest possible forms of torture and execution. Philosophy professed to arm the soul against these dire contingencies, and the remedies it offered were as dire as the evils against which they were directed. And those who taught this severe discipline were recruited as much from the Epicureans, the advocates of laxity and voluptuousness, as from the Stoics, who preached the most rigorous moral restraint. Curiously enough, it was the Epicureans who showed the greatest enthusiasm and, one might almost say, heroism in this battle against pain.

Their method was simplicity itself: they refused to acknowledge that pain existed. Seneca, who belonged to the opposite school, marvelled at their paradoxical position. "To think," said he, "that anyone could cry out 'I am happy' in the midst of the most terrible tortures! But this phrase was heard in the very school of voluptuousness. 'This is the last and happiest day of my life!' said Epicurus, though suffering agony from a retention of urine and an incurable ulcer in his stomach." Is it not sheer bluff to assert that pain is nothing but a word? Is it possible to abolish pain merely by denying it? Anyhow, only very few can possess the necessary courage. In such a contest the majority of mortals are beaten in advance. Even the choicest spirits can resist only up to a certain point. To say the least of it, it requires physical energy sufficient to preserve the tranquillity of the soul in the midst of the worst sufferings, or, if we are less ambitious, to react against them, which, of course, is far from annihilating them. However, education and training can help us considerably in this respect—and, above all, a certain organic insensibility, a certain lack of nerves. The Chinese and the Japanese bear suffering far better than we. Do they manage to abolish it entirely solely by strength of mind, even when committing hara-kiri, which supposes real moral nobility? It seems highly doubtful.

What is indisputable is that pain can be resisted. This resistance, which apparently is rarely crowned with victory, can give rise to a pleasurable pride in feeling oneself so strong. And this feeling of strength can, to some extent, distract the victim from his suffering.

My friend Joachin Gasquet has entitled one of his books *Il y a une Volupté dans la Douleur* (There is a certain Pleasure in Pain), and he does his best to demonstrate the paradox. It is quite possible eventually to enjoy suffering to some extent. Even Plato made the observation that very little separates pleasure from pain, but the pleasure Gasquet has in mind would seem to be of a purely negative character, merely a *façon de parler*. It is just the proud joy of denying suffering. The important point is to know just how far this denial or resistance is effective. I remember how Gasquet used to laugh at my complaints and expostulations about the cold, or the heat, or fatigue, or any other discomfort. Whether soaked to the skin by rain, or whipped by the icy blasts of the mistral, or broiled by a midsummer sun, he was always cock-a-hoop and offered himself exultantly to the uncontrolled fury of Nature. He had his way of saying "I am happy" in the most trying circumstances, which was extremely irritating to his less resistant comrades. Later on, during a German air raid and in the midst of the mud, ordure, rotting corpses, and all the other horrors of the trenches, he maintained his equanimity, if not his congenital exuberance; and no one had his power of raising the spirits of his men. And yet this was the man who in his last illness twisted and turned and roared with pain. He suffered, notwithstanding his proud protestations to the contrary. His only retaliation was not to let himself be beaten. But he was determined to remain true to his doctrine. I have never heard anyone give the denial to pain more fearlessly than he. It did not exist, he said, so long as one did not allow one's mind to dwell upon it. . . .

* * *

Gasquet was an Epicurean. Many a Stoic might have envied him his constancy. Seneca himself acknowledged the reality of pain. "You must not think," he said to Lucilius, his disciple, "that I put the sage above humanity or that I deny to him the sense of pain as if he were a rock that had no feeling. I know that he is composed of two substances: one is unreasoning—that which feels wounds, burning, or other hurt—the other is reasoning. The latter has unshakable opinions; it is courageous and invincible. This is the seat of man's highest good. Before it is completely filled with this, the mind is fluid and irresolute, but when the task is finished it is fixed and immobile. . . ." All this is very excellent, but it does not do away with pain. Notwithstanding this rather pedantic display of constancy, the most that the sage can do is to watch himself suffering with equanimity. But he would do better still to divert his thoughts from his misfortune. "It would be good," concedes the philosopher, "to detach oneself from pain and turn one's thoughts to other things. Think of the honourable and brave actions you have performed, consider the noble rôles which you have played. Recall to mind the deeds you have particularly admired. The noble men who, in their time, triumphed over pain, will not fail to appear to you. You will see the man who went on reading while his varicose veins were being cut away, and the man who laughed without ceasing while his infuriated executioners used every instrument of torture on him."

How this, too, smacks of the lecture-hall! What hollow-sounding consolations! It would be better to admit that the sage himself is unable to forget pain, let alone deny its existence. After all, perhaps the best plan would be to defy it with all one's strength. "Struggle against suffering with all your strength of mind. If you give way, you will be conquered. But it is you who will be the conqueror if you brace yourself to meet it." But this stiffening of oneself cannot last for long. This intransigent attitude in the face of evil cannot be maintained. Therefore let us confess our weakness with a good grace. Let us not disdain to lower ourselves to the level of common prudence. Finally, then, the Stoic is inclined to think, with Cicero and the Academics, that we must resign ourselves to suffering. "If your pain is violent, it will be brief. If it lasts, it will be slight. If you feel it too much, you will not feel it very long. It will put an end either to you or to itself. If you cannot bear it, it will bear you off. . . . Remember that serious pain ends in death, slight pain has intervals of relief, and we can master the intermediate kind. . . ."

I greatly fear that this fine reasoning is not worth much when it comes to actual practice. And is it even true? Are we really the masters of ordinary pain? Even the slightest pain becomes intolerable if sufficiently prolonged. Think of the hair-plucking torture in Edmond About's *Le Roi des Montagnes*. It was bearable for the first ten or eleven hairs; after that the victim began to howl.

We see, then, that to conquer pain, or only to attenuate it, by means of reasoning, is a very hazardous proceeding. It is easy enough to compile an imposing list of philosophic or scientific reasons, but in actual practice most of us just submit to Nature—which not only interrupts the worst pains with periods of calm but allows the organism to habituate itself to them and thus to bear them. Almost invariably there takes place an instinctive adaptation. As the well-known saying goes, "one gets used to anything." Goethe considered this spontaneous adaptation of living beings to circumstances, no matter how unfavourable, as a law of Nature. In the same way as plants accommodate themselves to the most unfavourable conditions and eventually take those forms that suit them best, so

the human organism makes every effort to overcome deadly obstacles and eventually finds the
means to accommodate itself to them and to live in
company with them. . . .

* * *

But adaptation does not abolish pain; at the most
it only attenuates it. Therefore why not acknowledge
that in reality, in spite of all the specific palliatives
discovered by physicians, and the arguments put
forward by philosophers, there is no remedy for
physical evil?

Christianity is well aware of this. For Christians,
as for Schopenhauer and his disciples, pain is the
law of life. To live is to suffer; to suffer is to live.
If it is impossible to destroy pain without at the
same time destroying life, there is no other choice
but to utilize it, by considering it as a means of
asceticism and detachment—detachment from this
life of suffering so as to attain a higher life, which is
peace through renunciation of the world.

For the Christian, suffering is, first of all, one of
the forms of charity. It leads him to a greater love,
in making him one with the rest of suffering mankind, in associating him with the sufferings of Christ,
who is the living symbol of human suffering as a
whole. Finally it leads him to renunciation of the
world, to conversion, that is, the re-turning to God.
He reascends to the heights from which our first
parents fell, he mounts the steps of the lower life and
turns towards the life of grace, which is the true

life. He may continue to suffer in his body, but his soul is profoundly joyful at feeling that the more he suffers the more he is detached from the life below and the nearer he is to God. It is what Pascal calls "the truly Christian state: to suffer in the body and to be comforted in the mind."

Suffering thus resolves into tenderness, into love for others and for God, into renunciation and quietude, into confidence and illuminating faith. But what a price has to be paid for this consolation!

It will be objected: "That is an heroic state. It is very few who can raise themselves to such a state of virtue." But no! The humblest of good women are equally as capable of attaining it as Pascal, or St. Teresa. . . .

CHAPTER III

THE GARDEN OF AGONY

AFTER having considered the question of grave natural pains, we would do well to turn our attention to all the other varieties of pain that lie in wait for us, namely, accidental, and what may be termed artificial pains, those which result from accidents, or which are inflicted on us by the hand of man, or which we bring upon ourselves: the sufferings of operations, of corporal punishments, all the sufferings that we have to fear from the cruelty of our fellow-creatures.

All of us are liable to the most painful accidents, and all of us are more or less likely candidates for the operating table. Even corporal punishment is becoming once again a disagreeable eventuality for which it would be prudent to prepare ourselves. We have a deplorable tendency to persuade ourselves that all the old atrocities, all the old social iniquities, from which we have been freed, have disappeared off the face of the earth. We give no thought to the fact that slavery still exists in its most primitive and harshest form, and not only in the darkest depths of Central Africa, but in countries that present all the external attributes of our own civilization. We forget that men and women are still put to death on account of their religion or merely for an expression of opinion; that intolerance and arbitrariness, once so hotly denounced by our Encyclopædists, are spreading right across the globe —from Mexico to Moscow, and from Moscow round again to Mexico, taking in their stride all the barbarities indigenous to Asia, Africa, and Oceania.

Any day we might be captured by Berbers, Moors, Tuaregs, Arabs, or Chinese, either when bearing arms against them or through the breakdown of our aeroplane or motor-caterpillar—and die a most fearful death. Any day the Bolshevist prisons may open their gates to us and their executioners subject us to the most refined tortures. Nay, that marvellous régime may take up its abode in our very midst: the masses would soon relearn the cruelties that are supposed to be sunk in perpetual oblivion. Let us not be under the delusion that the Garden of Agony is permanently closed. Unfortunately this is far from being so. That garden is no sadistic fantasy created by a diseased imagination. On the contrary, now is the time to recall the words: "It will always be approached by a thousand different paths. . . ."

* * *

First of all, there are the beneficent executioners —I mean the operating surgeons. Are their operations always painless?

An eminent surgeon, Dr. Louis Prat, of Nice, writes to me as follows:—

"Generally speaking, painful operations are a thing of the past; modern surgery looks on it as a sacred duty to do away with pain, by means of either local anæsthetics or artificial sleep. Besides, it would be impossible to operate on a patient who fought or struggled. The only painful treatment that is still employed is the setting, without anæsthesia, of fractured and dislocated limbs. It is still practised on occasions because it means only a few seconds' suffering. An *accouchement* is another extremely painful proceeding. Then again in a case of a purely local anæsthetic, a patient with a lively imagination or sensibility can, if he follows the operation in his thoughts, experience suffering that is real enough—in fact it may be actually physical."

There is no doubt that individual sensibility plays an important part in operations. The worst patients, it appears, are the doctors and surgeons themselves, nurses, artists, and brain-workers. To gauge the patient's powers of resistance one ought to know his race and nationality. Thus the Jews, an ancient race with a refined or decadent sensibility, are extremely sensitive to pain. People from the north of Europe bear pain better than those from the south or east—and the Italians less easily than the French. Finally, age and sex must be considered. Women bear pain more easily than men. On the other hand, old men are more resigned. The easiest patients to operate on are children.

In the psychological sphere there is a great diversity of phenomena. "Some patients come to the operating table with a feeling of deliverance," almost joyfully in fact. Some are calm and resigned; others are nervous and agitated. And there are some—their numbers are dwindling, we are told—

who display a senseless, completely unreasonable panic. . . .

"Immediately after the operation, most patients are happy to find that what they had been dreading so keenly has taken place without so very much trouble after all, and they think that they are definitely cured. They are quiet, full of confidence, and proud of having undergone the operation so successfully, especially if it was a major one. They describe it in full detail to their relatives or the patients in the beds on either side of theirs. In the public hospitals, the men ask for a cigarette or a shave, the women for their powder puff and lip-stick—all of which signs are looked on as excellent by the surgeon.

"In this respect, too, reactions vary according to race and nationality. The Anglo-Saxons, for example, do not want to know anything about their operation. They want no explanations: it is something extremely disagreeable that is finished and done with. They do not want to think about it any more. The French, on the other hand, are curious to the point of indiscretion and childishness—and they always want to see what has been removed from them. . . ."

Finally, needless to say, every surgical operation is faultlessly performed, to the honour and glory of the surgeon and the well-being of the patient.

* * *

But if the operation itself is nothing, the consequences are usually very painful and long drawn out. And it is not always the most difficult and dangerous operations that have the most painful aftermath: physical suffering, moral suffering, the whole gamut of suffering. One of my friends who for some time past has been engaged in what are known in Christian circles as 'works of mercy' has allowed me to make the following extracts from her notes.

"At the Hospital of St. Roch at Nice was a working lad, fifteen years old, who had his thigh crushed. He was operated on, and on coming to, he complained of a violent pain in his knee. The nurse said to him: 'Something wrong with your knee? . . . Have a look at it!' And throwing back the bedclothes, she showed him that his leg had been amputated. The poor boy had such a shock that he fainted right away and very nearly died.

"During the War a young fellow, completely crumpled up, said to me: 'I was operated on this morning. . . . I came to before it was over, and they couldn't get me off again because they had run out of chloroform'. [This did happen sometimes.] 'I felt then, and have felt ever since, such a terrible pain that I can't make the least movement. I can hardly breathe'. His eyes were haggard, and he spoke in broken sentences.

"The most awful expression of suffering I have ever seen was on the face of a soldier who had had both his feet amputated as a result of frost-bite. He persisted on going downstairs with a stick in each hand, walking on his two stumps, which evidently had not properly healed. When he got to the bottom he collapsed. He had fainted away with pain.

"Another wounded soldier who had had his leg amputated told me that his artificial substitute gave him such agony that he often had to stop in the street and lean against a wall for fear of losing consciousness and collapsing on the pavement. Another man who had been wounded—this time in the war of 1870—was suffering from anchylosis and had no control over one of his legs. His story was very similar: 'For the last twenty-three years I haven't been out of pain for a day, no, not for an hour. . . .' "

To counterbalance these sad cases, there are some patients who never feel a thing, either before or after the operation. "A young Italian girl, eighteen years old, with a beautiful head and shoulders, had slipped and fallen underneath a tram. Both her legs were amputated from the waist downwards, and that was followed by further surgical treatment, for the terrible wounds kept opening. She had been a domestic servant in a middle-class home at Nice, and she was visited by her employers and her friends, who brought her flowers, chocolates, scent, ribbons, and other knick-knacks. With a mirror in one hand, and a comb in the other, she arranged her hair coquettishly, laughing and joking as she did so, and thoroughly enjoyed visiting days. She was perfectly happy, as far as one could see. And then, in accordance with the hospital regulations, she was sent back to her home. This meant, first of all, a railway journey, then a ride in a farm-cart along a rough mountain road from the station to the village. The wounds reopened, she lost quantities of blood, and she died before reaching home."

The situation, then, as regards operations and their ensuing complications, is very much the same as in the case of serious illness: only a partial suppression or deadening of the pain is possible. And here again spiritual remedies are more effective than material ones. A distinguished university professor wrote to my friend: "For years I have been undergoing operations, and I have had to endure unspeakable pain without cessation. If it were not for my two children being dependent on me, I wouldn't stand it." A skilled workman who had been either wounded or poisoned in the War, told me personally: "They took away part of my stomach. The operation lasted nearly an hour. I had only a local anæsthetic, so I was conscious all the time. I had no physical suffering, only mental. I saw and heard everything. But I wanted to live . . . for the sake of the children."

It seems to me that only strength of will or some supernatural aid can enable us to survive such trials as these. Otherwise, there is nothing for it but to writhe and howl like a wretched animal. And now we will turn to the question of corporal punishment and execution. . . .

* * *

The point to be considered is not whether we are to be impaled by Celestials, slashed to pieces by Tongking pirates, decapitated and mutilated by Berbers or Moors, or whether we are to have our bellies slit and our bowels removed by Bolshevist— as not so long ago in England by Tudor—executioners. These delightful eventualities are always possible and more or less close at hand. What we have to consider is how and up to what point the victim can withstand these paroxysms of suffering.

We will leave on one side those who give in immediately, whose only tactics are to weep, scream, and struggle, like Mme du Barry when she was taken to the guillotine. She rang the changes on weeping and raging; at one moment she was biting the executioner's assistants, at another she was plunged in despair. It is probably victims of this type that suffer most of all; they touch the extreme limit of fear and horror. We will consider only those who accept the trial, either resignedly or actually with joy.

Again due regard must be paid to the sensibility of the victim, which varies according to race, nationality, and social status. We are told that the reason why the Chinese have such cruel and refined tortures is because they have no nerves: they have to be put to the worst tortures in order to suffer at all. I am not sure that I agree. It may be that their apparent insensibility covers a very real strength of mind, a moral capacity for resistance likely enough in the case of a race with such an ancient civilization. Over here, the coarsest, least nervy, folk are the most fastidious and the least able to bear suffering that is at all acute and lasting. Whatever may be the reason, the fact remains that the Chinese, even the lowest classes, when put to the torture, make it a point of honour not to cry out or to give any other sign of suffering.

And yet the punishments they undergo are both terrifying and abominable. The Republic has officially abolished them—some concession had to be made to European prejudice—but they are still carried out more or less openly throughout the country. Until recently they were public functions. Report has it that the punishment dreaded most by the common people was that by fire. The criminal, or victim, was burnt alive in this ingenious fashion: "The condemned man is tied to a stake"—so we are told by an eye-witness[1]—"and is left there naked all day long. At nightfall three pints of petrol are poured down his throat, followed by a long fuse which is forced down into his belly. The fuse is lighted, the petrol catches fire, and the victim explodes in one great burst of flames, to the huge delight of the assembled populace."

The same witness describes at length another form of execution that is even more intolerable to our Western sensibility. In this case the victim is gradually cut to pieces. We will pass over these horrors quickly; the mere idea of them makes us shudder and arouses our disgust and indignation. We will just give a thought to the instruments of torture, the assortment of knives, which in themselves are works of art and in the hands of the executioners take on a sensibility and a sort of devilish intelligence. The breasts are cut off the living victim like slices of meat . . . then his biceps, the arms, the buttocks . . . and all these operations are performed with a cunning slowness. Then the elbows and knees

[1] Cf. Louis Carpeaux, Pékin qui s'en va (Paris, Maloine, 1912).

are broken at the joints, and the limbs are thrown to the dogs along with the pieces of flesh that the poor wretch has seen sliced off his own body. . . . What ignominy! . . . And yet our forebears tolerated equally revolting spectacles in our public squares, and our people feasted their eyes on them!

One of the chroniclers of Lorraine, Philippe de Vigneules, has preserved for us the shocking memory of a similar execution that took place in the fifteenth century at Metz, just in front of the cathedral. One of the inhabitants was cut to pieces in the Chinese way, with all the most unimaginable protractions and refinements of cruelty. But we need only remember the famous executions of our regicides, such as Ravaillac and Damiens: the red-hot pincers, the molten pitch and sulphur poured into the wounds, the hand burnt on a brazier, and finally the wheel and the tearing off of the limbs by four horses! . . . We might remember also the fearful cry uttered by Damiens when they brought the burning brazier near his hand—a cry that petrified the mob assembled in the Place de Grève. Nevertheless, both Damiens and Ravaillac showed extraordinary courage during the whole of their long and ignominious torture. Of all these victims the most astonishing by reason of his calm and apparent insensibility was Balthasar Gérard, the murderer of Prince William of Orange. His odious task accomplished, his conscience at rest, he died like a martyr, fully convinced that he had performed a holy deed.

At first sight, the case of Gérard seems incredible, so incredible that certain prejudiced historians have had to have recourse to 'scientific' reasons to explain it. Just think for a moment. The wretched man was first thoroughly whipped five times by a row of men armed with rods; then he was smeared with honey and delivered over to a goat with "a right rough and hungry tongue," which was intended, while licking him, to take off skin and flesh together. Next, he was slung up with weights to his feet, and pierced with needles. After that, lumps of flesh were torn off him with red-hot pincers. Then his hand was burnt in a waffle-iron held over a fire; but he uttered no such terrible cry as escaped from the lips of Damiens. When this was over—he still maintaining silence—he merely raised the stump of his hand and regarded it—so we are told—with an air of proud composure. This resistance to pain, that might well be termed heroic, dumbfounded the spectators. "Never in my life," attested a contemporary witness, "have I seen such determination and constancy in a man. Not once did he cry out with pain. He went through every torture without a word, just praying beneath his breath, as one could see from the moving of his lips." Another witness states that "when they were tearing the flesh off his limbs he not only did not utter a cry but did not even murmur. This made the Dutch believe that he was possessed by the Devil, and the Spaniards that he had Divine assistance."

We are assured by experts that such cases as these have been "scientifically defined and classified to their total satisfaction." And people who pride themselves on being able to provide an explanation for everything calmly maintain that these cases are on a par with those of fakirs, Aissaouas, and dancing and howling dervishes. But even these are difficult to explain on purely physiological grounds. It must be remembered also that these charlatans or professional sufferers undergo a long training and progressive hardening. There was nothing like this about Balthasar Gérard and others of his type. He was just a simple visionary, but a visionary sustained by an ardent faith, a faith that drove him to commit a crime. He looked on himself as a martyr, and he was seen to die with a prayer on his lips. It was his faith, his faith alone, that rendered him, not insensible to the most fiendish torture, but capable of bearing it without a murmur.

The case of the authentic martyrs is analogous. I say 'authentic' because among these 'athletes of Christ', as they used to call themselves, there were many who were nothing more than maniacs, crazy visionaries, whose excessive zeal and extravagance had to be kept in check by episcopal authority. Could it be said of the authentic martyrs that they were mentally diseased or that they were pseudo-sufferers who, like the Aissaouas, had undergone a long period of preliminary training? Official documents and eye-witnesses' accounts rule out any such assumption. We have only to read the 'Passion' of St. Blandina or that of SS. Felicitas and Perpetua to see that they were perfectly normal creatures, leading, before they were torn away from it, an ordinary existence, with nothing remarkable about them except the ardour of their faith—three very youthful women, physically rather delicate and therefore the easiest of preys to pain. Against torture they had no defence except this ardent faith. This was their 'sedative', this was what others seek in some hopeless philosophy. A great hope filled the hearts of these tender women. Thanks solely to this spiritual strength they held out to the end. This is what Pascal considers to be the truly Christian state: "To suffer in the body and to be comforted in the mind."

* * *

There are all sorts of courage: individual, collective, active, and passive. . . . We may be capable of one and completely incapable of another. He who is apparently a coward on the field of battle may be a hero on a bed of agony or the rack. And *vice versâ*. Witty remarks used to be passed about the Italians of the nineteenth century who had lost the habit of collective courage: "It makes no odds whether you dress them up in red, green, or blue," said the French soldiers of their Neapolitan confrères, "they always cut and run." And yet these men who cut and ran had individual courage to a supreme degree. Stendhal, who knew them well, admired in them not only their individual courage but their sense of honour, which they cultivated to the point of folly. They accepted challenges to duels that would have made the bravest Frenchman hesitate. The defenders of Saragossa could not withstand a modern army in the open, but behind a wall, or man to man, they displayed amazing audacity, intrepidity, and contempt of death; there has never been a more sublime resistance.

Active courage has something animal about it; it is composed principally of heated blood and ignorance of the danger. But it may also be deliberate, in which case it is akin to passive courage. It consists then in advancing coolly in the face of a danger that is fully realized, in accepting an unavoidable eventuality with tenacity of mind and in staking everything, even life itself, in order to triumph over it.

Passive courage is insufficiently esteemed. Its heroism is less conspicuous, but it is, in most cases, more meritorious. To remain inflexible when undergoing torture, or prolonged and hopeless suffering, demands a fortitude that would be quite beyond the capacity of many a reputed hero. This fortitude is of a purely spiritual nature.

The Stoics used to recommend suicide in cases of prolonged and intolerable suffering, but for torture they had no other remedy than *aequanimitas*, evenness of mind. Is that sufficient? Not in my opinion. We need also a *strength* that is capable of simultaneous endurance and resistance. The Stoics thought to draw this strength from the feeling that the sage, having attained this high degree of impassibility, became the equal of the Deity. But is it possible? I feel surer of finding help in Christian hope and in a firm resolution to cast myself entirely on God's charity. Many of the martyrs believed that it was Christ who was suffering in them and for them, and from this 'consolation' they derived unheard-of courage.

A possible objection is as follows. In order to suffer less, we ought to be wholly absorbed in God, but may it not be that suffering, prolonged and accentuated to the point of paroxysm, turns our thoughts away from God? Philip II, in the midst of the torments with which we are acquainted, begged for a respite in his death agony so that at the last he might belong entirely to his Maker. It is certainly a very troubling thought. It seems likely, however, that these respites, even though they be of only a minute's duration, are always granted. It may have been during one of these moments that William of Orange's assassin was able to contemplate the stump of his arm and wonder what had become of his hand that had been burnt away in the executioner's waffle-iron. However that may be, nothing is seen to have a more soothing effect in such cases of extreme suffering than the hope, or the certainty, of supernatural aid. There may be other aids at which human pride is capable of grasping, but whatever we do or think, we must feel that we are being sustained by something that is stronger than pain and death. It may be an idea, it may call itself God, conscience, deliverance, or redemption. There is no other remedy than this strength that springs from the depths of the soul or comes to us from outside. And do we not feel at certain moments that we are raised up and fortified by something that is not ourselves, by a great unknown force, superior to that which tortures us and kills us?

CHAPTER IV

THE MISERY OF LIVING

HOW do our individual sufferings stand as regards pain in general? All the teaching of philosophers reduces itself in the end to the pessimistic formula: to live is to suffer, to suffer is to live! Similarly, all the morals pointed by our preachers are nothing but a paraphrase of the *vanitas vanitatum* of the Scriptures, the world considered as a "vale of tears."

"If we had before our eyes," says Schopenhauer, "the horrible pains and sufferings to which life exposes us, we should be appalled. Take the most confirmed optimist by the hand and conduct him through the hospitals, the sanatoria, the operating theatres, the prisons, the torture chambers, and the dungeons. Take him to the battlefields and the places of execution. Show him the murky lairs where poverty lies hidden, shunning the prying glances of the stony-hearted. Finally, let him take a look at Ugolino's prison in the Tower of Hunger, then he will see what his 'best of all possible worlds' is like. Whence did Dante derive his conception of Hell if not from the actual world in which we live? . . . This world, this scene of carnage, where fear-stricken and tormented beings subsist only by devouring one another, where every beast of prey is the living tomb of thousands of its like and sustains its life only at the expense of a long line of victims, where the capacity for suffering increases in proportion to intelligence and consequently attains its highest point in man. . . ."

The first fault to be found with this gloomy picture is its incompleteness: whatever Schopenhauer may have to say, pleasure is as positive as pain. It is not merely the absence of pain; it has a quality, an intensity, a savour, of its own. Living is not only suffering, it is also loving, understanding, doing. No doubt, his reply to this would be that the least effort or the least change in condition of the mind involves pain. But it is also accompanied by pleasure—and this the pessimist refuses to acknowledge. His sombre picture is merely an arbitrary conception, which may always be countered by a totally opposite conception—an optimistic conception of the world, the sum total of all the joys of which every human life is, to an appreciable extent, composed. The sum total of good or ill looms large or shrinks according to the frame of mind we happen to be in. Were we to submit the question to one who calls himself an average man, a man in the prime of life, free, or nearly free, from infirmities, whose secure existence has not hitherto been marred by serious accidents or disease, who is as confident about the future as he is about the present, who shares all the advantages of a solidly established society and civilization—almost certainly such a man would give it as his opinion that we are never either as fortunate or unfortunate as we imagine ourselves to be—and that, taking it all in all, life, if not exactly good, is at any rate 'well worth while'.

* * *

It is no less true, however, that this average conception of life presupposes a rather too liberal quantum of obliviousness. To be of this opinion a man would have to forget that he is an exception and that there are millions and millions of people in the world who are dying of hunger and cold, who succumb to overwork, who are withering away in poverty, exposed to every calamity, to every physical and moral contagion.

In the Sahara there is a particularly barren and desolate region, of no mean size, known as the Land of Thirst. The Land of Hunger is considerably more extensive: its boundaries embrace the most fertile regions of the globe. We who have seldom had to miss a meal from the moment we were born never so much as even think of it; we have no conception of it. Which of us ever gives a thought to the ravenous and almost incessant hunger of the Hindu, the Arab, the Bedouin, the Berber—one might almost say three-quarters of the wretched inhabitants of the globe? To hideous, emaciated Famine, dying on the roadside, piling up corpses by the hundred? Who thinks even of those who are starving in our very midst? We would rather not believe that such a thing is possible. It goes without saying that in a country that has long been christianized and civilized no one has to suffer from hunger, let alone die of it! And yet . . . the friend of whom I have spoken, the friend engaged in works of mercy, has some heartrending tales to tell me in her letters. From among the most normal, the least upsetting, ones I select the following: "One of the poor families I visited at Nice consisted of a widow with sixteen children of her own. Her husband had been a mason. This is what she said to me: 'Yesterday I had nothing to make a fire with. I put some bread on a dish with a little salt and vinegar. The children ate it up' [she still had four of them left], 'but since my husband died I have never had the joy of hearing them say that they had had enough'."

The same lady writes to me about the frightful scenes of destitution in the slums of London, where the entire population of certain quarters suffers not only from hunger but from cold, dirt, and disease, the last being brought about by the condition of the hovels and by every kind of vice, the most ravaging of which is drunkenness. Here is a description of her visits: "In this home the children wake up in the morning to find that there is nothing left for them to eat, and so they stay in bed. And what a bed! . . . At another place a little boy has died. I saw him in the cellar where the family live, the mother dealing out slaps and punches to her six young children who were fighting and crying round their little brother's corpse. . . . There was a moving scene at church. Everyone kneeling on the ground —dockers, ragpickers, beggars with the look of convicts—and all of them put money in the plate. Sometimes the women kneel down at the altar rail and say a short prayer. The priest makes the sign of the Cross on their foreheads—they have made a vow to keep sober for three months. A longer term of engagement, being impossible of fulfilment, is not accepted. . . . Some of the few husbands who were sober, but whose wives were not, were doing the day's shopping. Hardly had they come home and gone out again to work than their wives went out and raised money on the meat, the fish, the sugar, or the tea. In their husbands' absence they left their children in bed and foregathering in one or other of their hovels drank until they were rolling on the floor."

In the midst of all this degradation there are some wonderful examples of devotion to the poor. Again I quote my friend. "At the mission in London I knew a young nun, twenty-eight years old, who was dying from heart disease. As I was accustomed to retiring late to bed, it was no trouble for me to sit up with her till two o'clock in the morning. She suffered terribly from difficulty in breathing and incessant vomiting. She never complained. 'An English woman', she said—not a Christian woman, mark you—'does not complain'. She wanted to go on living so that she could continue to sacrifice herself for others. She was looking after a group of factory girls. 'I wanted to do so much more for them!' . . . She died a few days after I left London."

* * *

It is always possible, if not always easy, to remedy this kind of poverty and suffering. Sometimes material help is all that is required; at other times nothing can be done but to contain one's soul in patience. I mean now the evils of war, of industrial, and even climatic, conditions. This planet of ours is far from being habitable for all. We who live in temperate climes, in the midst of a class of humanity that has had the spirit of altruism inculcated into it for centuries, with all the conveniences and refinements of a highly developed culture—we, I say, have no idea of the hellish conditions of existence in certain parts of the world, in particular the areas under colonization: India, Arabia, the equatorial regions of Africa and America, countries like Alaska, that border on the polar regions. . . .

Algeria, even the southern portion of it, is a paradise in comparison, and yet quite a large selection of tortures awaits the European in the Saharan regions: overwhelming heat suddenly following on cold spells that are often very severe, ubiquitous dust, insects, reptiles, rodents, brackish water, loss of appetite, everlasting thirst. When my lips are parched and cracked, when the sand accumulates beneath the door and the pustulous and voracious lizards begin to run along the rafters, I know that I am in the South, and I resign myself to all its plagues. But these are mere trifles compared with the hardships, the hostility, the natural scourges, the diseases, the degradations of every kind that afflict the colonist in Western Africa. The books written by Robert Randau, who spent several years in these inhospitable regions, give us an inkling of the nature of colonial life.

He describes the terrifying fauna, the gigantic vegetation that both overwhelms and poisons human beings, and, worst of all, the diseases and vices engendered by the climate, the semi-barbarous, putrefying atmosphere.

The winter is possibly even worse than summer, torrid though it is. "For the white man in a tropical town, winter is the season of fear. He is haunted by the thought of yellow fever, plague, intestinal disorders. He watches the departure of the mail-steamers, their prows turned towards the north, bound for Europe. With a sinking heart he mutters to himself: 'Another two years of this for me! Shall I be able to stick it out until I am due for leave again? Ah! To think of my friends drinking their cool, fresh beer in the cafés! Little do they realize how fortunate they are!' And dragging one foot after the other he wends his way back to his house. His bedroom is like an oven. The boy has forgotten to air the rooms in his hurry to get away and dance to the rhythm of the tomtom. The sheets are clammy. As darkness falls, the mosquitoes, scenting fresh blood, set up their indefatigable buzzing. The bats beat their wings against the blinds. The beautiful sleep he was going to have till dawn—he knows now that all hope of it has gone—and the next night will be the same. He gropes his way to the bath and sluices off his perspiration. Hardly has he dried himself than his skin begins to itch all over and suddenly breaks out into thousands of painful little pimples. He is in despair; there is no remedy to stop the itching; it will go on until the coming of the dry season—three months more to wait."

Petty troubles, perhaps, but in course of time they become an intolerable torture, and they are only the harbingers of worse calamities. "What a prospect for the colonial in the tropics! The bouts of fever, the interminable hæmorrhages, the black vomit, hæmaturia, parasitic diseases. . . . And with all this, premature decay; old age at thirty-five; sickly children. A pleasant outlook!"

The most terrible disease of all is yellow fever. . . . One day, without warning, the medical officer, on taking his place at table, having just completed his round, announces that some cases have been discovered in the neighbourhood. "No one asks the doctor whether the cases in question have proved fatal; we all know that there is no cure for this disease. A clot of blood forms in the bladder. One expires in an agony of eructation, with a final black vomit. Careful measurements are taken of the victim at the first definite signs of the disease, so that the carpenters can set to work on his coffin right away.

". . . The wasps buzz round our heads, and some of them drop into our plates. A silence has fallen on the party; one or two have grown a little pale; a slight constriction of the throat deprives them of their appetite. A brief shudder runs through the group of whites, a shudder such as ran through the dancers of the Red Death at the striking of the hours —that sinister dance described by Poe. But the Red Death slew its man in a few moments; the Yellow

Death takes three days to drive its victim out of existence. During this lapse of time a horrible, acute pain hammers on his temples and wrings his liver and entrails, and turns his spine into a rod of red-hot iron."

Further, colonials die young. . . . "Genuine colonials hardly ever live beyond the age of fifty; one has only to look at the statistics. But we might as well quit early! During our youth and middle age we are away from civilization, away from everything that is good and beautiful, far from our family, our relations, and our friends. . . . I loathe Africa, but I cannot bring myself to leave her. She is a mistress that refuses to be shaken off, and that is all there is to it!"

* * *

The man who said that is an old pioneer with an intimate knowledge of his fellow-men. They are capable of suffering the colonial atmosphere until it kills them. They hate Africa as the cause of all their troubles and their degradation, but they are desperately attached to her.

With them it is primarily a question of habit. To hark back to what I have said already: *One gets used to anything.* But the words must be taken in their deepest and most tragic sense. It is the progressive adaptation of the plant to the most pernicious conditions. At the bottom of the heart, or the mind, of all these men—soldiers, missionaries, colonists, civil servants—there is one idea, one faith, especially, that keeps them going: civilization, the redemption of souls, the victory over barbarism.

Moreover, there is the joy of understanding, the joy of action: the joy of understanding something that is not us, that runs counter to our mode of life and ethical principles, and, above all, something that challenges our intelligence . . . and action, merely for the intoxicating joy of action, for the consciousness of increasing will-power. . . .

This certainly cures no evil, and it can offer us but feeble aid in our struggle against the pain of the world in all its manifestations. But it enables us to keep going, as they say. Whatever suffering it may be, we have always, eventually, to fall back on the two great, the two sole, remedies: physical courage and strength of mind.

CHAPTER V

MISFITS

I SHOULD not like to say which kind of pain is worse, physical or mental, but it seems to me that the intellect and will find less difficulty in reacting against the latter. An illness or an accident can suddenly turn us into a groaning, moaning, delirious mass of flesh and bones. On the other hand, the possibilities of mental suffering are infinitely more numerous.

Leaving on one side the commonest known, the most banal, varieties, those which immediately occur to the mind, we will concentrate on the sufferings of those who have failed to adapt themselves to their surroundings. These sufferings are infinite in number, and many of them are indistinguishable, so subtle are their differences.

Some suffer from a hostile milieu, either of a material, social, or family nature. Let us begin with noises. The suffering caused by noises is more intellectual, or mental, than physical. The infernal din of modern mechanical appliances makes life very hard for those who have need of silence and solitude; the wireless, the gramophone, the roar of motorcars and aeroplanes, the ear-splitting rat-tat-tat-tat of road drills, make life impossible for the man who wants to think and meditate. What remedy can be offered to these brain-workers whose nerves are set on edge far less by the torture inflicted on their ears than by the feeling that their thoughts, their imagination—that which is of supreme value to them, that which they hold most dear—is at the mercy of some banal street noise or the whim of an idiot? Not only are they humiliated at being held of no account, at being reduced to impotence by the most insignificant of obstacles, but they are genuinely distressed by the stupidity that inflicts such an utterly useless torture on them, at the inanity and barbarity of human beings who need to distract themselves by means of this frightful racket. Street noises, noises made by our neighbours, give rise to the most pessimistic reflections on human folly.

Lack of solitude is even crueller. It is one of the worst tortures of the Bolshevist inferno. I am not surprised that people of refinement who have been condemned to a life of promiscuity should be so disgusted by it as to have recourse to suicide. Nor is there any need to have come down in the world in order to suffer from disharmony with one's environment. The same hostility, or lack of understanding, is found among people of the same class, of the same education, of the same family.

Just as I did not choose to be born in such and such a class of society, I did not choose to be born in such and such a family. What consolation can you offer me if I have nothing in common with those of my own blood or my own class, if I feel more estranged from my associates or my blood-relations than from a Polynesian or a negro from Central Africa? I have known more than one child who seemed to surround itself with a wall of silence and to be in a perpetual state of self-defence—and savagely at that. Was it the clumsy treatment of its parents, their inability to handle a rather tempestuous or sensitive nature? Very possibly. Roughness on the part of a parent, a harsh word, an unmerited reproach, may consummate the spiritual divorce between members of the same family. The wound inflicted on a child's feelings may never heal. The child who is cowed will always be cowed, no matter what may be done to bring it out of its shell. The saddest part of all is that there may be equal good-will on both sides. But the points of contact have gone for ever. They have no feeling for each other, they fail to understand each other, they don't speak the same language. Consequently, they resign themselves to isolation. A wall of ever-increasing thickness is built up between the person affected and those around him, and this may be the cause of great suffering on both sides.

* * *

There are some people who are so objectionable to us that their company causes us actually physical suffering. They are so obstructive and malevolent towards us that they upset our equipoise and exasperate us to the most intense degree.

A girl once spoke to me thus about her mother: "I have no particular reason for disliking her, but I just can't stand her. . . . She seems to have some electric force contrary to mine. The mere fact of her being in the same room with me makes me feel uncomfortable."

And the girl who told me that was a charming creature, very kind and very popular.

The reasons for an antipathy of this nature—a natural, not a spiritual, antipathy—are lost in the depths of the subconscious and in the mystery of heredity. But the reasons for other antipathies are obvious: the coarseness of some people is so palpable that it sometimes causes physical discomfort, a discomfort so irksome that flight is the only remedy. Contact with certain moral taints chokes us like a noisome stench.

On two occasions in my life I have been reduced to tears by particularly heartbreaking instances. They were literally 'enough to make one weep'. Was it because their stupidity assumed fantastic proportions in my imagination or was it the purely physical effect of their presence? The fact remains that as I could neither run away nor control my nerves, I suddenly burst into tears, to the blank astonishment of the other person, who was in the middle of a funny story. . . .

Luckily, this has happened to me on only two occasions, for it is quite an humiliating experience.

* * *

Certain interior awarenesses are still more irritating.

It is not easy to explain the matter clearly. As the mystics say with reference to one or other of their states, "one needs to have experienced it." What I am thinking of is the presence within ourselves of a being that is at the same time both alien and similar to ourselves. It is as if we had a double personality. We feel that we are dominated by a will and a mentality hostile to ourselves and to the persons that we love most—or rather the persons that we want to love most. And at the same time we feel that we ourselves are this intruder who sets us at variance with ourselves so obstinately that we despair of ever setting things to rights. We feel this identity profoundly, and yet at the same time we say to ourselves: "That is not I! I hate this interloper! I don't want to have anything to do with him!"

The physical counterpart of this phenomenon is very common and very well known. Without any doubt we carry about with us a horde of ancestral ghosts who fight among themselves for the possession of our body and our facial features. Take a long and careful look at yourself in a mirror: that face of yours which you thought you knew so well will dissolve into a crowd of strange faces and assume an expression you have never seen before. First of all you will see pass before your eyes a gallery of ancestors whom hitherto you have known only by their portraits. In you, they are living, they are continuing their lives. There are the eyes of one of my grandfathers: they look at me through my own, which are so like those of his portrait that I can no longer find my own expression. That is my father's profile, and that is my mother's; they have come out of my profile and have finally appropriated it for a fleeting second. There are moments, too, when we see the lineaments of a relative long since disappeared or dead pass across the face of a brother or sister, like the diaphanous clouds that float across the disk of the moon and seem to vary its physiognomy. And if you continue to stare into the mirror, there will be presented to your eyes another series of faces that you have never seen before, faces that have taken the place of yours—that is to say, the face you think you know—faces that gradually dissolve under the fixity of your gaze. . . .

We are more or less conscious of all this, just as we are conscious of our spiritual resemblance to our forebears. We are not at all surprised to find ourselves reproducing this or that trait of our father's or mother's character or any of their physical traits or blemishes—it is a matter of common experience. But what is strange and inexplicable is that we carry about with us the souls—or the halves or portions of souls—of strangers. A being different from us, a being that contradicts us and torments us, is installed in the most obscure region of ourselves, like a monster at the bottom of a well. We are aware of the monster's presence, we know what it is capable of, and we know, too, that it is alien to us only in a certain sense, for we have a deep-seated feeling that it is ourself, that it is our flesh, our blood, our feelings, and that sometimes it mixes itself up with our thoughts. And yet it is contrary to us, it is continually acting in opposition to our wishes, it sets us at loggerheads with our conscience. It is an enemy; it torments us cruelly. This being, that seems to be the manifestation of what is most instinctive in us, can be childish, capricious, extravagant, absurd, blindly obstinate. Against our will it makes us commit innumerable acts of folly; it makes us cruel and inexorable when we want to melt into kindness and affection. It makes us deaf to every reasonable remonstrance, it petrifies us into a state of stupid inertia when we long to give ourselves entirely and follow the dictates of our heart. It causes us indescribable suffering to be at the mercy of this diabolical being. I call it 'Mara' because the bitter, gloomy sound of the name seems to express as well as anything the fundamentally evil nature of this demon we carry about within us.

* * *

Worst of all is when our 'Mara' has fallen out with that of a person whom we love or whom we want to be able to love.

A friend of mine who is of a sentimental nature, though outwardly the opposite, sends me the following pathetic confession:

"There is one person whom I have wanted to love above everything—that is, above every other human love—to love absolutely, without reserve—and whom I still love in spite of everything that separates us. That person is my mother. It began as soon as I was conscious of my own existence. Instinctively I wanted to nestle up to my mother's heart. I wanted to find shelter and comfort there. The love between a mother and child seemed to be so much above all other loves, so much purer, so much more disinterested—a love such as one might have for God. It is the last rung of the ladder that leads to Him. Love for any other woman is so adulterated with selfishness and baseness: 'Love me, since I love you, or I will kill you!' We demand immediate and, so to speak, tangible payment for the affection we have expended. We demand nothing of this sort from a mother. We can go on worshipping her without receiving anything in return. . . . But the fearful part about it is that we cannot tell her what we feel. Mara erects an impassable barrier between two persons, one of whom at least wants to be able to love the other with all his heart.

"It began with little irritations: an unfortunate word or action, a phrase not in any way hostile in itself, or even disagreeable, but sufficient to betray a profound difference of soul. Some sentiment or idea which was not to my way of thinking shocked and wounded me deeply, not because it humiliated me but because it lowered my idol in my estimation. And I was utterly dejected and desperate at feeling myself so far away from the person I loved —so far away in fact that we would never be able to meet again, except possibly for a few brief moments of emotion when it is more a question of flesh and blood than of soul. And so I drew further and further away from her who was so dear to me, although she had no idea of what was happening to me and I would have given everything I had for her heart to be nearer mine. . . .

"The years passed, and other loves claimed the attention of my adolescence and maturity, but my affections were misplaced, and the result was utter disillusionment. I turned for comfort to a surer love; I went back instinctively to her whom I had never ceased to cherish. Once again I tried to establish connection between two souls that sought to find themselves in one another. . . . It was impossible. Mara was there, thwarting every attempt at reconciliation. Mara is a fury that may relax her vigilance for a moment but she wakes up at the slightest sound coming from outside, and putting out her claws she hurls itself at her counterpart in the being that is dear to us. Notwithstanding all our efforts to restrain them, the two furies remain sworn enemies. How did they come to us? Who put them into us? Who is it that makes them so hostile to each other in the case of two persons of the same flesh and blood? They are always there, like two dogs, each behind a gate or fence, ready to bare their fangs and to tug at the chain, at the first sound of a footstep on the highway. . . .

"Anything sets them barking: it is one perpetual irritation and misunderstanding. It is not the slightest use our being on our guard against the stupidity of the beasts; it is no use trying to check them with our reason and our need for affection. Every attempt at explanation fails: our words betray us and are taken in the wrong sense by either side; instead of pacifying, they only irritate us further. Speaking for myself, this feeling of impotence drives me to despair. It's like an immovable weight on my chest. I want to cry out my affection; but an indomitable power paralyses my being and seals my lips. Mara is there, to defy my reason and my will."

* * *

On reading these lines I asked myself whether Mara was not a pure phantom created by an author's imagination or by the tendency we all have, more or less, to dramatize ourselves, to 'play to the gallery'. After analysing this peculiar condition of the soul, I used to form a fantastic conception of it; Mara took shape before my eyes as a mythological monster. But now it is no more than a residue of obscure heritages that set us violently at cross-purposes with analogous heritages co-existing in ourselves or in others. There is nothing like sifting one's ideas by process of analysis.

But whether we analyse it or explain it, we are arguing from the unknown to the known. Perhaps the true Mara is at bottom the mysterious being that frightened me at first; the Mara brought to light by my analysis would be only a feeble imitation, an incomplete reconstruction, lacking, among other characteristics, the quintessence of malevolence or diabolism inherent in this demon of anarchy and mischief. It makes no difference: in spite of all these restrictions and attenuations it is a power which is only too real, and we have to reckon with it.

Mara has a crowd of relatives who might easily be mistaken for her sisters, but it would be inaccurate to identify them with her. *Les Hommes de Lettres*, a curious romance by the brothers Goncourt, is a lengthy study of a case that is very similar to Mara's. Their hero, the over-sensitive Charles Demailly, an amateur playwright, marries an actress in whom he hopes to find the ideal companion for a man of letters: "Soft, infinitely soft, sympathizing with our fancies, an inexhaustible source of attention, both soothing and reanimating, the mute attention of a mother, for what are we but children? . . ."

He imagines her to be not only kind, but refined, as he is, appreciative of every form of art, and clever. But before long, when the sensual excitement has died away, he finds that she is exactly the reverse. First and foremost, she is stupid: "My wife is a ninny, a pretentious little ninny who gives you the impression of having brains. She has the worthless sentimentality, and all the prejudices, of the *petite bourgeoisie*. She dotes on everything I detest. Everything I despise, she reveres. And she's not even good; she thinks of nothing but herself, her dress, her appearance in the world. She is malicious; she knows all the things that touch me to the quick and she goes out of her way to make me suffer. She does this with a hypocritical gentleness, with an air of pitying condescension, as if I were an invalid that needed humouring. At other times her vanity comes into play, and she tries to show me how intelligent she is, and how great an artist. She forces herself to admire things she neither feels nor understands, and it is then that she is quite intolerable. She's like a musical instrument that grates on one's nerves, that is always out of tune. . . . No! I'm through! She makes me suffer too much! I feel that she loathes me with every atom of her being!"

But this is merely a collision between two fundamentally hostile temperaments. It is not the doubling of personality that characterizes what we may call the 'Mara complex'. It is not two real beings that oppose and attack each other in the persons of Charles and his wife. Both remain true to their own ego. The wife's may momentarily conceal itself under a veneer of convention, but it soon makes short work of this veneer. The artificial character with which she masks herself is not in violent conflict with her true character. On the contrary, the real ego, for reasons of vanity, summons the conventional ego to its aid. It is in league with it.

Things would fall out differently if Charles and his wife were subjects of a Mara complex. The wife would be neither irritating, nor stupid, nor malicious. She would have all the gifts and qualities fit to charm a man of letters. She would also have all the affection and devotion necessary to soften and soothe the most delicate and susceptible soul. But between Charles and his wife there is Mara, the genie of discord and hatred, who by some mysterious trick of heredity has taken up her abode in the soul of one of the couple, or possibly in both. Mara will poison their relations, and exasperate each of them against the other. Charles loves his wife as he would a mistress, the ideal mistress. But he cannot prevent himself from keeping a secret watch on the woman he adores, with the unacknowledged desire to find her at fault and prove her inferiority. She always does the wrong thing. She never knows when to appear or vanish opportunely. She never knows when her presence is unwelcome. He listens to her speaking, he watches her walking, he watches her eating: everything she says is futile; she is heavy, utterly graceless in her gestures, and bestial in the way she attacks her food, in the way she puts a spoon into her mouth. He tries to make her understand how much this pains him, but he is so upset that he cannot find the words he wants. She takes offence, and the argument becomes envenomed. Both have the feeling that, for the moment, they are under the domination of an evil force that perverts their thoughts and prevents them from finding the words to bring about a reconciliation. Defeated, they resign themselves to retaining their unexpressed feelings within their hearts. As heavy as tombstones, bouts of silence fall between the two beings that long to come together but feel they will never succeed in doing so. . . .

Charles ponders over the hostility he has discovered in his mistress—an hostility which is groundless but which he feels to be impregnable. And he says to himself: "There is nothing to be done. She detests me, in spite of herself. She can't help detesting me; it's in her nature to do so. And I can only love her by deluding myself. What I love in her is the person I want her to be—the person she forces herself to be, just for my sake. She's acting a comedy for my benefit! But it's a horrible farce! If only she would go, and put an end to it!"

And so they separate. But hardly has she gone than Charles is in despair again. He accuses himself of stupidity, injustice, weakness, lack of will-power. "Good Heavens! Don't I know her faults? Can't I put up with them, seeing that I love her—and she loves me, and I am sure of it? Am I not a Pharisee, am I not inhuman, to expect her to conform in every detail to the arbitrary image I have formed of her? Can't I forget all that and concentrate on one thing—the fact that we love each other?"

He makes his apologies and eats humble pie. She comes back, and they both agree that they have wronged each other. But Mara has not disarmed herself, neither on his side nor on hers. On the first possible occasion the vicious beasts leap over their fences and fly at one another's throats. The torture begins again. . . .

* * *

This kind of love makes the mistake of seeking a perfection that is not to be found in this world. If we suffer from this misfortune—I mean the misfortune of being unable to resign ourselves to the vexations and hostilities that are inherent in another person and in ourselves—we suffer also in overcoming our repugnance. And yet we must attain this end; and we do attain it by force of will. The will is always the supreme court of appeal. We suffer in having to will against our own nature and against the nature of another, but this exercise of the will is also a joy and a consolation. We will suffer, then, and console ourselves in willing not to suffer any more, neither on account of others nor of ourselves, until we have the courage to turn towards the threshold where pain expires, the threshold which is also the entrance to the only Love.

CHAPTER VI

THE INCONSOLABLES

THE Inconsolables are misfits of a special kind —the hopeless kind.

Love-sickness, home-sickness, heaven-sickness: these are the signs by which they may be recognized. This is how Lamartine describes the hero of his *Raphael*, who is an inconsolable misfit: "The distinctive trait of this child's character was a feeling for beauty both in Nature and in art so vivid that his soul was practically nothing more than a transparence of the material or ideal beauty distributed throughout the works of God and man. This originated from such an exquisite sensibility that it was almost a disease with him until time had somewhat toned it down. We used to speak of him of having 'heaven-sickness', in the way that other people suffer from home-sickness."

It is the disease of the Romantics: a vague longing for other places, for some indeterminate good, some indeterminate happiness not in one's possession, a loathing for all one's surroundings, for men and for life in general, together with the fearful certainty that there is no means of escape from such an existence. Romantic nostalgia is hopeless, and it takes a pleasure in despair, for it regards it as a consolatory distinction and elegance. This is where the disease of Romantics differs from the nostalgia of the mystics, who also suffer from 'heaven-sickness'. The latter, however, want to be consoled; they insist on hoping to the end. Even when enduring the worst forms of physical suffering, the worst spiritual trials, they refuse to be discouraged, for they know that they will see God. They even ask for more suffering, so as to make themselves more worthy of Him. To suffer in body and soul is to purify themselves in preparation for the final union. Not that they look on God as a Moloch who must be fed with human pain. No, it is because they know that the infinite number of pleasures that drag man down must be counterbalanced by an equal number of sufferings, by means of which man is detached from the world, raised up, and redeemed.

St. Teresa suffered cruelly in her body. She accepted it and even rejoiced in it as a painful but necessary cure to complete her rupture with the earthly life. She tells us that the sufferings most difficult to bear are those of the soul deprived of God, the periods of abandonment and 'dryness', as she calls them, when the Beloved does not respond, when the tired soul becomes indifferent to everything, even to God's silence, when it is not even strong enough to want Him. And just as she experienced inexpressible joy in being united with her God, so too she suffered untold tortures in being deprived of Him. But this dryness and abandonment are never permanent; hope always returns eventually. She knew that even in her crises of discouragement she was obliged to hope and that to fail in this theological virtue would have been a grievous sin.

* * *

The saints have no need of our commiseration. The really unhappy people are those who suffer without hope: the unconsoled and the inconsolable. Probably the most incurable are those who have been wounded by love, those who are delivered over to all the madness of a hopeless human love— a misdirected love, for real love can have only God as its goal; it goes back to Him who is its source.

A love deceived, a love broken off by death, by an irreparable misunderstanding, by a separation which may never end—these are the usual causes of this fatal malady. There are those who cling dementedly to this senseless thing, who wear themselves out in trying to perform the task set as a punishment to the Danaïds: they cherish the worship, the ever-present illusion, of a hopeless love. To think of it unceasingly is their only joy, their only consolation. To evoke the past, to try to resuscitate it, to deceive themselves into a belief that their beloved image is living flesh and blood, when they are certain—only too horribly certain—that this dead image will never, *never*, come to life again ... such remedies are no better than morphia: they become more and more ineffective and intensify the suffering.

Such experiences are common. Here is a case that is more out of the ordinary run of things. A woman of my acquaintance, of no great culture, it is true, but extremely emotional beneath an undemonstrative exterior, found herself in the following situation. After having been madly in love with a young man who had died before his time, she married, on purely rational grounds, a rather ordinary man, of feeble character but very good-hearted, very much in love with her, who put up with her whims and outbursts without a murmur. She had several children by him, and as far as the world could see she was living in perfect married bliss. Actually, however, she could not forget her youthful love and the death that had been the great drama of her life. It took on a more and more romantic aspect in her memory. For years she hid her inward suffering, this perpetual, silent nursing of her pain, and then one day, on the death of her youngest daughter, a child of twelve, for whom she had never shown any great affection, there was a sudden melting into tears, a sudden demonstration of an inconsolable and unreasonable grief. Every day she was at the cemetery, crouching over the grave of her little daughter, heaping it with flowers and wreaths. There she used to stay for hours on end, bathed in tears and sobbing violently. Her secret sorrow that she had held in check so long and had disguised so jealously had burst its barriers. She utilized her daughter's death as an excuse for coming out into the open and weeping out her soul at long last over the person she really mourned, her dead lover who became more and more alive the more she cherished him in her memory—the man to whom she dedicated every day long, silent hours of reverie. . . .

In the case of one who was so sensible, so self-controlled, such a display of grief was inexplicable. Her acquaintances concluded that she was stricken with remorse and that she realized at last how remiss she had been in the treatment of her daughter. No one had any notion of what was really happening—not even her husband, who eventually gave up all hope of getting to the bottom of her extraordinary behaviour. She used the occasion to make the poor man's life unbearable, flying into a passion about everything and nothing, the result being that he understood her less and less. It seemed as though she were avenging herself on him for the long constraint she had endured and the disappointment caused her by her marriage.

Meanwhile, she suffered terribly. In the first place, she was ashamed of this playing to the gallery. She knew quite well that this outward grief of hers concealed another, incurable grief, the pain of which had been revived and had burst forth with renewed fury under cover of this mourning for her child. And then in the end the two griefs coincided, each one stirring up the other. She managed to persuade herself that the true cause of all her tears was the child whom she regretted not having loved sufficiently. But she could not act this lie for ever: her only love, her real love, re-entered her heart and overwhelmed and obliterated every other feeling; it was more obsessing, more tyrannical than ever. Wrapped in her grief, rejecting every consolation, every token of sympathy or affection, she died only a few months after her little daughter. . . .

* * *

The torture of cherishing a hopeless love is doubtless even more poignant when the beloved one is still alive, when he or she is there, quite near you, only a step or two away, and yet completely unattainable. It brings to mind the song of the Fates in Goethe's *Iphigenia*, the tragic contrast between the torture of Tantalus, the unquenchable thirst of the Damned, and the profound tranquillity, the unassailable felicity of the Immortals, who look down from their golden thrones on the painful and purposeless agitation of us humans. For such an affliction there is no solution but a miserable death or madness.

It is useless to reason with those who are thus afflicted. The insanity of love has seized them in its grip and will never let them go. They are well aware that the insanity is fatal, but they cherish it more than life itself. They are possessed; the soul is dispossessed. They can no longer hear at the bottom of their hearts the saving Word: "You would not be seeking Me had you not already found Me." . . . They do not want to seek, they do not want to find. "What need have I of your God? Your Eden holds no joys for me. Nothing interests me now except my love. What does it matter if I die of it?"

And they do die of it. But the pity is that before this happens their suffering is long and cruel.

* * *

However, though the victims themselves may have given up all hope, we can always go on hoping for them. There is always hope that the time may come when they will realize their folly. Also, it seems that mental suffering is less independent of our will than physical suffering, the causes of which are beyond our comprehension. There is always hope that the former may be remedied by a sudden effort of the will, a revolt and a stiffening of the vital instinct, illuminated and spurred on by the conscience. In the case of physical suffering there is often nothing to be done. Physical evil is a worse scourge, and more humiliating for us, than mental trouble. Science may do all in its power to push back the frontiers of pain; it always has vast territories and lairs from which apparently it is impossible to dislodge it.

The older we grow the more we appreciate the fact. Let me repeat: a painless old age would be, taken all in all, acceptable. Who would not resign himself to growing old were he certain that he would not have to suffer? But as the years go on, our sufferings increase. Let us suppose an old age free from the more grievous ills—which actually happens more often than we think—there is still the inevitable procession of infirmities that are more difficult to bear than grievous pain, by reason of the continuity of the suffering. It is this feeling of the perpetual presence of pain that imparts a bitter flavour to the utterances of the aged. A perpetual menace is upon them, and by their slightest words and actions they transfer its gloom and terror to everyone with whom they come in contact.

This, no doubt, is why homes for the aged have always filled me with repulsion. They are homes for sufferers. Some of them are nothing more than human rubbish-heaps, jails for the dying. In others, the inmates are provided with every possible comfort; but however luxurious may be their quarters they know that when they leave them it will be feet foremost. Listen to the tone of voice in which they tell you: "This is the last lap!" This feeling of approaching death would be nothing were it not for the infirmities which diminish and debase them in their own estimation and make them unbearable both to themselves and others. Hence the desperate longing to be gone; hence the appeal to Death, the deliverer. . . .

As I write these lines my memory recalls the image of my mother, who was nearly a hundred when she died but who had retained, as they say, the full possession of her faculties. Besides the infirmities which are inseparable from old age and from which she suffered cruelly, she was prey to an unconquerable lassitude, an oppression of soul rather than of body, as if the weight of years were not merely a gloomy metaphor for her mind, but something very heavy, a material weight that was crushing her. Together with this there was a sort of shame at the futility of her life. This idea was profoundly humiliating to one who had always been so active. Though not aware that she was doing so, she was continually repeating the words uttered by

St. Monica on her death-bed: "*Quid hic facio?*"—
"What am I doing here?" . . .

I always picture her as I used to find her in her
room when I came upon her unawares: sitting
motionless in her armchair—pale, with a pallor
that contrasted lividly with the intense blackness
of her locks, which had lost none of the colour they
had had when she was only twenty . . . her face
rigid, with an almost cadaverous rigidity, already
lifeless and ossified, already returned to its mineral
nature, like a human ruin. Her eyelids closed, her
hands joined, she was ready for the grave. But under
the goad of suffering her veiled eyes reopened.
They were the only living organs in the whole of
her lifeless body. In their poignant look were concentrated all her feelings and all her thoughts,
which were possibly more vivid, more ardent, than
they had been at any previous period of her life.
It was the final blaze of a dying fire, an ebullition
of consciousness at its maximum intensity. With a
look of supplication she would contemplate a
crucifix that she had had placed on a chest of
drawers in front of her, and from the movement of
her lips I surmised that she was uttering this inward
monologue: "My God, deliver me! What am I doing
here? *Quid hic facio?*" . . .

This is the benefit of pain: it softens the frightful
passing. It even makes us long for it. It leads us
imperceptibly to the threshold that we cross once,
never to return. . . .

PART III

DYING

"How can you prove that death is not an evil?"

SENECA
Epistles to Lucilius.

CHAPTER I

MY MENTAL BACKGROUND:
THE HEIGHTS OF THE ESCORIAL

I MUST admit that for this final meditation on death I found it rather difficult to choose a local background. I have endeavoured to give to each of these meditations a setting which is not only analogous to the subject but which is really suggestive or symbolic of a complete order of ideas and which even reveals aspects that were—to me—either entirely new or unsuspected. Casting my mind back, then, to the places I have visited in my time, I sought out one that would not only be appropriate for such a serious subject but would also be revealing. . . .

Naturally enough, my thoughts turned first to the apocalyptic Valley of Josaphat, which the blood-curdlers of the Middle Ages selected as the site for their descriptions of the scenes that were to take place at the Last Judgement: graves reopening at the sound of the Angel's trumpet, the Son of Man sitting in the clouds, the thousands of millions of dead converging from the east and the west, the north and the south, the bottomless chasms of time and space. But these colossal imageries would overwhelm the little depression of the Cedron, that meagre, stony bed of a torrent that is nearly always dry, an indentation that has managed to usurp the name of valley only by a trick of rhetoric. The exiguousness, the dull grey poverty, of that celebrated spot was one of the greatest disappointments of my visit to Jerusalem. To make matters even worse, in an attempt to brighten up the miserable Jewish cemetery, the authorities that be have succeeded in vulgarizing it. Gardens have been laid out with herbaceous borders, pots of flowers, and artificial ponds that only need goldfish. No, it was impossible to think of death in this sprucely-kept, commonplace, insipid spot.

Another site of terror claimed my imagination for a moment: the no less celebrated Valley of the Kings, which lies among the mountains dominating the course of the Nile and the classic plain of the hundred-gated Thebes. This and the Dead Sea are the two creations of Nature in the Near East that have left the deepest impressions on my memory. The Valley of the Kings is an awe-inspiring entry into Hades. There is nothing to equal it in Virgil, or even Dante. To experience the horror of it to the full, it should be entered under the blazing sun at noon. The sinister, shadeless funnel, apparently devoid of vegetation, the perpendicular streams of tawny rocks, which shine with a metallic lustre like walls of copper, the terrifying shaft, whose edges, of almost geometrical straightness, cut into the hard blue of a cloudless sky—it surpasses any scene imagined in a nightmare. . . . And then, suddenly, after these solar incandescences and dazzlings, the burning atmosphere that has become so heavy and oppressive as to be almost material, comes the descent into the icy gloom, the opaque, interminable blackness of the funerary cave, amid the cabalistic paintings revealed at lengthy intervals by electric lamps fixed to the passage-walls . . . figures of monsters, of animal-headed gods, and, above all, of reptiles, whose coils unwind themselves like an endless cable through all the ghastly compositions. . . .

How repugnant the whole of this mythology is to us, with its overwhelming mass of detail! How remote from us is this ancient Egypt! And what a gloomy conception of the future life! The complete destruction, the annihilation, of the human being would be preferable to this precarious survival, this depressing immortality: a life of night-watchings, a Cimmerian life with all the needs of earthly life, insufficiently satisfied by images of food and servants, and the perpetual threat of unknown horrors! Ah, no! Let us turn our thoughts away from this odious nightmare, these mummies swathed in stinking bandages, deprived of their entrails, their heart, and their brains, these scarabs, these Osirises, these amulets with magical inscriptions, all these lugubrious devilries, and all the maleficence that floats in the fetid air of these coffin-glutted hypogea. . . .

* * *

And so my thoughts returned to the Escorial, firstly on account of an old predilection for what has always seemed to me to be the most symbolic, the most expressive, monument of the Spanish character and genius; secondly, on account of the current prejudice to which Barrès has given its definitive form, as Chateaubriand did for the Dead Sea, to wit, that the Escorial is a mortuary locality where one cannot do aught but meditate on death and one's ultimate destiny. This is Delrio-Barrès' conception of it as exemplified by his *Du Sang, de la Volupté et de la Mort:* "This landscape, tortured by sombre passions and dominated by the royal monastery as by a crushing slab of granite, seemed to him to be just the sort of setting that a meditative Pascal would present to his imagination in order to crystallize it." In other words, the Escorial is, for him, the symbol of a terrifying, Jansenist, conception of death.

Barrès never troubles himself about what places actually are and what they signify. He uses them as a background for certain states of mind, and he makes them conform to his own and serve as pretexts for his meditations. We have every admiration for his fine temerity, to which we are indebted for many beautiful passages of prose, but in our own case we shall be more humble. We shall endeavour to efface ourself in favour of the object, solely interested in the thing itself and what it signifies. . . .

* * *

Well, then, here I am again at the Escorial-on-High, as the Spaniards call it, in the little hotel where I stayed on my last visit. It commands a most extensive view of the plain of Castile, and in clear weather one can see, at the extreme limit of the horizon, the blurred white mass of the Royal Palace at Madrid. Once again I marvel at the austere but magnificent landscape.

On the day after my arrival I pay my respects to the Rector of the University which has been established in one of the subsidiary buildings of the monastery, and to my friends the Augustinians who are in charge of the famous library founded by Philip II, who celebrate the Mass for the Dead, likewise endowed in perpetuity by the same monarch, and who edit the scholarly Augustinian review of theology, philosophy, and history entitled *The City of God*. The great African, the author of the *Confessions*, is a bond between us.

On emerging from this home of erudition, I turn about for an instant to contemplate the court in which the edifice is framed on the west and north. Known as the Lonja, this vast quadrilateral, paved with slabs of marble-like granite, forms in conjunction with the classical orders of the principal façade a supremely distinguished ensemble, superbly Spanish in character. . . . Then I climb the escarpments of the mountain by little zigzag tracks as far as the platform on which have been placed the reservoirs that supply the monastery and its gardens. Straight in front, shaded by the overhanging rocks and foliage, the basins gleam sombrely, like great mirrors of ebony; at my feet stretches a vast expanse of country, undulating like the sea, the background merging into the greyish sky—it is the plain of Castile, as bare and tawny as

173

a desert, in which the Escorial, with its white walls and domes and its green *huerta*, orchards, and pleasure gardens, takes on the semblance of an oasis. Seen from above, the Escorial is indeed an oasis in the sand, a place of well-being and refreshment—the *refrigerium in Domino* of the early Christians—and it was conceived as such by its founder— a place of refreshment for both the body and the soul.

But this was only one of his leading and inspiring thoughts; the charter of foundation mentions others: to build a temple of granite to the glory of God, as Solomon did, and thus show his gratitude for the victory of St. Quentin and the preservation of Catholicism in his realms, so that it should be not only a temple but also a triumphal monument (the four enormous pillars supporting the dome are known as the *Triunfo*). Finally, to inaugurate a pantheon in the vaults of the basilica where his father, the Emperor, the members of his family, and his successors should be laid to rest. These were Philip's original intentions.

Subsequently, his project grew. The Escorial became a monastery, for monks were necessary for the service of the dead as well as for the service of God. But Philip desired that the monks should serve the living, too. Not only were they to preach and evangelize, but also to educate. Their convent was to be a university and a library, a source of light. It was also to be a hospital, a hostelry, a pharmacy, a laboratory, a *conservatoire* of sacred art, painting, sculpture, metalwork, needlework, tapestry, and so on, a school of liturgy, and finally a place of beauty and delight, and—as it still is for the Madrileños— a country retreat during the hot season. The Escorial was to ensure the service of the living as well as the dead; it was to satisfy all the needs of man and life. . . .

* * *

From the start, the monks looked on it from the same view-point as their founder, and firstly as a place where one is well looked after. This is borne out by the descriptions given by their annalists, in particular Father Siguenza. They are amazed at being so well accommodated, at inhabiting a con- vent that was at the same time so pleasant and so elevating, so suitable for praying—for one must be comfortable to pray. True enough, they admit that the winter is hard there—they are more than three thousand feet above the level of the sea—and that there are fearful winds and storms, but they have the sun at every season of the year, and the air is delightfully cool in summer. Good air, a healthy situation, pure water in abundance, springs, foun- tains, running water everywhere, and all the fruits of the earth, ponds full of fish, woods full of game— the cenobites would indeed have been ill-mannered to complain. Their cloisters and their cells were not merely everything they could reasonably desire but were actually magnificent. (I am speaking of the time of Philip II.) Their annalists go into raptures about their spacious ambulatories, the patios gay with flowers and gushing fountains, the princely staircases, the frescoes spreading along the walls and stretching up to the ceilings of the domes. "The refectory," says Father Siguenza, "has five large windows on the south side, flooding it with light and gaiety. Moreover, they cleanse it from every unpleasant odour, so that the refectory is as sweet-smelling as the sacristy." The enthusiasm of the good religious does not even stop short of the privies. "Their cleanliness is amazing," he confides in us, "and on every side there are water-channels in abundance. One may enter there without repugnance, and even linger there awhile."

As for the cells, the king's munificence and thoroughness were such that he gave them his personal attention. With his royal hands he placed a painting here and an engraving there, a chest here and a candlestick there, so as to bring out the full effect of every work of art and display it in its most favourable position. Just as his great-grandson, Louis XIV, imposed beauty on the members of his court, so Philip imposed it—and cleanliness—on his monks. And just as Mme de Maintenon, an incurable *bourgeoise*, grumbled about her sovereign's æsthetic whims—"He would make you die symmetrically if he could!"—so the monks at the Escorial cavilled at the superfluous splendours of their convent, at everything that the king imposed upon them merely on the score of beauty. On the other hand, they were unanimous in their admiration of the gardens, which were very different in their days from what they are in ours. They fall into an ecstasy over the great east terrace, the colossal platform where nowadays there is nothing to be seen but box-shrubs arranged in geometrical patterns, but which, in their time, was enlivened with running and spurting water, and was covered with flowering plants and trees, Spanish flowers, exotic flowers, rare plants of every kind, many of them from the Indies, the quantity and quality of them being such that in his enthusiasm the good Father Siguenza compares the terrace to the Hanging Gardens of Babylon. It is the same with the orchards and the parks, with their fruit-trees, their arbours, their trimmed hedges, their basins, and their monumental fountains, which were afterwards used as models for those at Versailles.

The austerity of the Escorial was thus tempered with magnificence and comfort.

* * *

This was the king's desire; it was his organizing and animating genius that made the monastery. On his retirement from the scene, neglect and decay set in, with the result that the Escorial of today has sadly altered since the time when Philip II spent several months there every year.

What was it that he sought there? Firstly, rest, as was only natural, seeing that he was overburdened with the work and worries incumbent on a sovereign whose rule extended over half the world. Secondly, escape from the midsummer heat that made a furnace of Madrid. Thirdly, and principally, the pleasure of seeing his architectural creation rise

from the ground and grow. Unable to construct
Europe according to his liking, he consoled himself
at the Escorial with constructions that satisfied both
his Christian sentiments and his artistic tastes or
idiosyncrasies. A collector and a lover of works of
art, he delighted in looking at beautiful pictures
and sculptures and in handling objects perfect in
their exquisite material and in their form. Though
thoroughly enjoying himself in this refreshing
summer-retreat, surrounded as he was by his own
creations and by beauty in every shape and form,
he conscientiously fulfilled to the letter all the irksome duties attaching to his royal estate. Spending
whole days at his desk, buried in administrative and
governmental correspondence, he had but little
time to meditate on death. As Bossuet was to say,
he both served God and ensured his own salvation
by the performance of his daily tasks.

But the few free hours that were left him after his
professional duties had been met he devoted to the
care of his soul, to the realization in his own person
of the Christian ideal, in so far as that was possible
for a king. The perfect life was that of a monk, but
the king of all the Spains, the master of the New
World, could not live a monk's life. However, he
would embrace monastic asceticism as much as he
could. Accordingly he was usually present with the
monks at office and he had his stall next them in
the choir. In the evening, in the well-known bedroom, which is nothing more than a cell, he read
pious books and indulged in more or less lengthy
meditations.

What was the subject of these meditations? That remains hidden in the secret places of his heart, but anyone who has the least acquaintance with him will be tolerably certain that he did not give over-much attention either to death, to our final destination, or to the misfortunes of mankind. He did not consider himself unfortunate. As a king, he considered that God had overloaded him with benefits; he even felt that to a certain extent he was personally associated with His grandeur: something of divine majesty attaches to the majesty of kings. Philip built his private apartments against the wall of the Capilla Mayor: his bedchamber was similar in character to the throne of the living God. It was because he was so great in the eyes of the world that he could humiliate himself in the presence of his God. As Louis XIV used to say: "Humility is a virtue more suited to kings than anyone," since they have some share in real greatness and thus have something to lower before the face of Him who is the greatest of all. . . .

Even if he was haunted by the thought of death and by the severity of the Supreme Judge, he saw therein no reason for despair. He quickly bethought himself of the infinite goodness of God and looked on death as the means of attaining eternal bliss. Death was not an end, a culmination; it was the entrance to everlasting happiness. He fixed his mind on the glory that crowns a life of penitence and self-forgetfulness. Just as his Escorial was but a cry of triumph to the majesty of God—"May God be praised!"—so a human life ought to be nothing

N 2

more than the striving after glory. In the famous painting by El Greco which is considered to represent a "Dream of Philip II" the king turns away from the horrors and the punishments of Hell and fixes his gaze upon the splendours of Heaven.

Certainly the thought of death was never far from his mind, as is the way with all of us; but for him death was but the point of departure for beatitude. It would probably be true to say that he had never been face to face with its physical terrors until the last six weeks of his frightful illness, but he betrayed no sign of fear, if fear he had, and he put forth every effort to present a smiling face. He breathed his last, holding between his fingers a candle blessed at Montserrat, the symbol of perpetual Light and Joy.

* * *

This is why I gladly select the Escorial as the background for this meditation; in the pages that follow, the thought of it will be, if not actually apparent, but lightly veiled. It not only provides me with the most appropriate setting for my subject, but it is for me a lesson in bravery in the presence of death. I have only to think of Philip on his death-bed, of the serenity he maintained until the end, of the almost joyful manner in which he left this earth, to be reconciled with death. As his biographers tell us, he takes it by the hand and presents it to us with the air of a sovereign, with the air of a master who has brought it under control. And he seems to say to us: "It's nothing! It's only another thing that I have mastered!"

The Escorial teaches me how death can be transcended by eternal life. We have not only to die, we have to live the whole of our life, our poor human life, which includes death itself, which is not complete without it.

This, then, is the lesson of the Escorial, with all the severity and the magnificence of its architecture, and of Philip II, with all the horror and the foulness of his death-bed: in the very midst of death, an exhortation to us to live a full life and enjoy unending bliss.

CHAPTER II

PLAIN SPEAKING

I HAVE just one misgiving. Is there not a risk that this preoccupation with the setting—which, however suggestive it may be, is, after all, external to the subject—may give a false note to my meditation by diverting it towards gorgeous fantasies, decorative images, which are no better than the allegorical figures and hollow urns that surmount a mausoleum? If there is any subject that demands entire sincerity, it is this one. It is not advisable to pose in the presence of death.

And yet no theme lends itself more readily to rhetoric, to every kind of artifice, to conventional explanations, and to literary elegance. The great danger is that we may delude ourselves into the belief that we are, in fact, sincere, whereas, without either desiring it or knowing it, we are only posing. Let us recall to mind one or two of the most celebrated passages from our Romantic poets:

> I salute thee, Death, celestial deliverer!
> Thou dost not annihilate, thou dost deliver us!
> Thy hand, celestial messenger, doth bear a torch divine.

The nihilistic apostrophe of Leconte de Lisle shows us the reverse side of the picture:

> And thou, divine death, to which everything returns and
>   is effaced,
> Clasp thy children to thy starry breast,
> Free us from time, from number, and from space,
> And give us back the rest that life has interrupted!

Then the note of despair, in Lamartine's *Novissima Verba:*

> And I too take my place amid the throng
> Of beings created and destroyed, who flee before thy face.
> I have seen, thought, felt, and suffered, and now I go,
> Dazzled by a lightning that is quenched for aye
> And saluting with a cry of horror, or of hope,
> The bank that I am leaving and that towards which I
>   plunge,
> As one who has been judged and irrevocably condemned
> To cast himself from the pinnacle of a tower,
> At the awful moment when his foot has left the height,
> Fills at least the abyss with one despairing cry. . . .

What splendid eloquence! Now and then pitiful cries are heard, cries of absolute sincerity, but again what rhetoric! Some of these tirades compel us to exclaim: "Bravo! This is lyricism put to galop time!" But the tiniest grain of fact would give us far more satisfaction. In a matter so unsettling as this, the least crumb of certainty would be preferable to all these rockets launched into the night. It is always the triumphal march for the death of a hero: the roll of muffled drums drowned in the blare of trumpets. . . . Even preachers are not entirely innocent of indulging in this empty show. For them, death is the entry into glory. Triumphal arches, set up on the threshold of Infinity, welcome the happy conqueror. "I envisage you as more triumphant there than at Fribourg and Rocroy. . . . Rejoice, Prince,[1] in your victory, rejoice in it for evermore!" Even though it is Bossuet who is speaking, we feel a little distrustful. It is all too beautiful, even for an

---

[1] The Prince de Condé, known as the Great Condé (1621–86), the subject of a famous funeral oration by Bossuet.

undeniable hero. It may well be that death is a deliverance, a victory, a triumph, but at what cost, how, in what sense? Is there not a danger that the grand words with which it is alluded to may mislead us as to the reality of things? I know that the funeral oration has its own laws, its own conventional flourishes, but leaving that aside, can we not reflect on death without these draperies, these funerary festoons? Can we not discuss it without adopting any of the conventional attitudes towards it, whether brave, indifferent, or despairing—without lying to ourselves?

* * *

Well, then, in the first place, what exactly is the subject under discussion? The glory, or the annihilation, that we hear about, is not death; it is that which follows death. And that is an article of faith. What we are interested in *first of all* is death itself. Similarly, therefore, we are not discussing what precedes death, the various stages of suffering and the final agony. That, too, is not death. What we mean by the word is the passing from life to a state of which we have no knowledge. Death is essentially this passing, and it is this that appals us on our first consideration of it. "To mitigate the horror of this frightful passing," says Lamartine at another juncture. It is precisely this that engages our attention, or causes us the keenest fear, since, for the believer, everything is decided by this passing, and, for the unbeliever, whatever happens afterwards is of no account. We shall not, then, enter into

purposeless discussions about "death's morrow."
No one knows anything about it, though whole
libraries of metaphysical works have been built up
on the theme. The teaching of the various religions,
including Catholicism itself, amounts to the affirmation of eternal bliss or reprobation, and beyond this
we are ignorant.

Do we know anything more about the passing
itself? To do so we should have had to experience
it, and those who have experienced it are cut off
from communication with us. Those who are in
process of undergoing the experience, that is to say
the dying, they, too, are unable to communicate
with us, or if they do make signs to us they are
incapable of expressing what it is they are experiencing. They let fall some vague words which are
more or less devoid of sense or which teach us
nothing: for example, "I am going!" or "It's all
over!"—which is perfectly obvious to us. . . . And
even those who have been in the very clutches of
death and have escaped, those who have actually
been 'between life and death', can tell us nothing.
The normal vocabulary breaks down when it comes
to describing such experiences, even though at the
time itself they were fully realized.

A similar incapacity is displayed by those who
have been the witnesses of death-scenes. What they
see or guess at is insignificant compared with the
mystery that is being enacted before their eyes.
Even the physical signs reveal but an infinitesimal
part of the drama that plays havoc with an organism
on the point of dissolution. What is happening to

the body almost entirely eludes the observation of the witness; still more so, what is happening to the soul. The long and short of it is, that we are left in utter ignorance. We must always be on our guard against historians, however matter-of-fact, and against pious annalists, who are apt to write their descriptions of death-scenes for the edification or instruction of posterity. And to this temptation we are all of us, involuntarily, inclined to yield, under one kind or another of unconscious influence. On re-reading the descriptions by eye-witnesses of the last moments of Philip II, I begin to wonder whether they were really as "joyful" as we are expected to believe. That he retained his courage, his resignation, his calmness, his majesty, is more than possible, but joyfulness?—that is asking too much. . . . And the same may be said of the death of Louis XIV. Here is Saint-Simon quoting from the diary of the Marquis de Dangeau, who affirms that these are the very words addressed by the dying king to his courtiers: "Gentlemen, I must ask you to forgive me for the bad example I have set you. I thank you for the way in which you have served me and for the attachment and the fidelity which you have shown. I am truly grieved at not having done for you all that I should have liked to do. Bad times are the reason for my failure. I ask you to have the same devotion and the same fidelity towards my grandson as you have had for me. The child shows every sign of eventually being able to surmount whatever obstacles may present themselves. May your example be

186

worthy of being followed by all my other subjects. Obey the orders given you by my nephew. He will govern the realm, and I trust that he will do so with success. I trust also that each of you will play his part in maintaining unity, and that should one of you depart from it the others will help to bring him back. I feel that I am upsetting myself and you. I ask your pardon. . . . Gentlemen, adieu! I trust that you will think of me from time to time!"

What nobility of soul, what an elevated style, and what magnificent simplicity! How courtly, how charming, that "Gentlemen, adieu!" But let us remember that it was a king speaking, not a dying man. Louis delivered that address five days before he died, when he still had all his wits about him. Moreover, there can be little doubt but that a man as meticulous as Louis XIV would have made a preliminary note of at least the essential points of that little discourse. In my opinion, the words spoken by the king during the last night of his life are more like those of a man who is really dying: "O my God, come to my assistance! Come and help me quickly!" And even this was only the prelude to his final agony. The actual death was hidden from the eyes of man. Whether it be a king or an ordinary mortal, the 'passing' remains a mystery. There are deaths that are triumphant up to the very last sigh. Would that all heroes and saints could die in this apotheosis of death! The Carmelites who assisted St. Teresa at her last moments expected her to make some revelations or at least utter some sublime, immortal words that would be handed down from generation to generation until the world should cease. She contented herself with recommending them to observe strictly the Rule that she had given them.

Then there are deaths that, though the dying persons themselves may not be disheartened, are disheartening for witnesses who are longing for light and consolation: deaths that are sad or gloomy, devoid of radiancy or fervour, walled up, as it were, within an overwhelming silence. And finally there is the scandalous variety: pious persons dying like the damned. Contrariwise, some pagan philosophers have died with serenity, if not actually with joy—Socrates and Seneca, for instance. But in the case of witnesses, their discouraging or scandalized impressions may be the result of preconceived ideas. They enter the death-chamber with their imagination in a fever: a hero, a saint, *must* die in such and such a fashion. It goes without saying that the virtuous will die with a smile upon their lips: "His end was absolutely peaceful. It was just the evening of a lovely day." All this is mere hallucination, misapprehension, or misinterpretation, on the part of witnesses who are either prejudiced or who have been insufficiently prepared. It is invariably the case that the brutal fact—the actual and simple fact—the actual passing or separation, eludes us. And it is no less certain that for the majority this passing gives rise to an unconquerable terror. We consent to dying since it is the inevitable end of human life, but the supreme moment, the final tearing asunder—may it not be such as to render all our other suffering insignificant in comparison? As in the dream described for us by Barrès, where he sees himself pursued by a pitiless executioner, we cry out: "I am willing! I am willing! . . . But do it quickly!" Alas, we cannot always be sure of being heard.

* * *

All that we know is that we shall have to undergo the passing at one time or another. As Pascal says: "The matter of which we know least of all is that very death which cannot be avoided." As far as our human intelligence can tell us, we do not even know if there is any reason for alarm. Perhaps it is not so terrible after all. Some people say that it is nothing. But there seems to be no hope of our ever having an irrefutable proof of the statement, and as long as there is doubt there is fear.

What attitude are we to adopt towards this doubt? Ah! If only our attitude could be thoroughly sincere, free not only from illusion but also from pose and bravado. Can we tell ourselves and assure others: "It doesn't worry me at all," when we know nothing of the danger to which we are exposed? In view of our utter ignorance, would it not be more judicious to prepare ourselves for an eventuality that is always possible and may be terrible? . . . We can prepare ourselves to meet a danger with which we are acquainted, and organize a defence against its foreseeable and always verifiable effects, but against a danger, a suffering, an evil, of which we have no conception, of which we know nothing except that it is not to be avoided, what preparations can we make, what remedies can we use? . . . At this actual moment, when my health is excellent, when I have complete control over my reason and my will, when I am borne along by the wave of life, I can say in all sincerity, because it is the inmost wish of my soul, the most imperious command of my conscience: "I shall be brave in the face of death." And yet how audacious, not to say presumptuous, is this valiant attitude! Who can say with absolute assurance: "I shall be brave on the field of battle"? Yes, certainly, at this moment, as I am fastening my belt, I can firmly and most sincerely desire to be courageous, but in a few minutes' time, when the bombs are dropping round me, what will become of this splendid resolution? It will be at the mercy of a panic, of a nervous failure, against which all the resolutions in the world are impotent.

Still more uncertain, still more chancy, is the attitude of the sick or dying person—unless he receives some assistance from outside, some physical, moral, or supernatural aid. When we are well we can lay up a store of courage, accumulate a whole arsenal of resolutions and splendid philosophical ideas, but at the last moment everything may vanish like a mirage. The firm resolution may turn into weakness and despair. At the supreme moment a new being, hitherto unknown to us, may spring into existence and derange our reason. Who can guarantee what he will be like at such a time?

Who can be sure of his will unless it be sustained by something stronger than itself? Even when we are in good health, are we not sometimes terrified by the alterative and subversive forces within us, by the instability, frailty, changeability of our ego? Are we to be accused of insincerity if, when it comes to the point, we belie all our former principles and with our own hands pull down the splendid structure of ideas we have erected in anticipation of the final crisis?

And yet we must vow to be sincere and courageous to the bitter end, in spite of all the treacheries of the body, the weaknesses of the soul, and the surprises that our death-agony may have in store for us. As for courage, that does not depend on us; but we can always promise ourselves to be true until the end. And in any case it will probably be easier for us to be so if we are in full possession of our intellect and will. It is less a question of attaining to an ever-elusive truth than of not letting words lead us astray as to our capacities and as to the result of our efforts in search of truth.

Once again: in a matter such as this, perfect candour is essential.

CHAPTER III

INSTINCT AND DEATH

WE will begin by defining the limits of the question.

It is agreed that we know nothing about the 'passing' and that we refrain from any speculation whatsoever about what follows it. We are to consider only death *in actu*, at the very moment of its happening. Though we may be in complete ignorance about the psychological aspect of the fact—which in any case is extremely complex—we do know that it is inevitable. Our task consists exclusively in determining how we are to comport ourselves towards this inevitable fact—not at the precise moment when it happens, for we cannot answer either for our reason or our will in a crisis which, it seems, must either suppress or transform our present individuality—but *from now onwards*, in anticipation of this thing which is equally fearful and inescapable.

Once again, all our preparations may be of no avail, and the attitude we adopt after careful examination and deliberation may collapse at the last moment. But that is not the question. We are concerned solely with our present conduct. Is it possible to calm ourselves from now onwards? Can we calm or discipline the contradictory movements of an instinct which at one moment goes frantic and

at another assumes a confidence that is just as
irrational as its panic?

* * *

To some people, death is nothing. It is just as
natural an event as any other; it ought not to disturb us any more than the fall of a leaf or the
bursting of a pod. To realize the naivety of this
conception it suffices to contrast it with others, such
as that held by Christian theologians since the time
of St. Augustine, namely, that death is a punishment
for sin.

In the naturalist conception, then, death has not
the importance that we attribute to it. It may be
noted, too, that both Asiatics and Africans regard
it with a splendid indifference. Gobineau, when
writing about the religions and philosophies of
Central Asia, lays frequent emphasis on the indifference to death displayed by the Hindus and the
Persians. In the same way, African explorers report
this attitude among Moslems and fetishists alike.
Neither Asiatics nor Africans can understand why
Christians, and Europeans in general, make such a
fuss about death.

There is no doubt that our European conception
of death is as far removed as possible from that of a
Parsee or a negro from Uganda, though some of our
Western philosophers, beginning with Lucretius,
have spoken of it with a detachment similar to that
of the most primitive populations, populations that
live most by instinct. Amiel has set down some
interesting thoughts on the subject, but they are

only a repetition of very ancient notions which are perhaps more forcibly expressed in the following passage from Buffon:

"Why fear death if we have lived sufficiently well not to fear its consequences? Why dread this moment when it has been preceded by an infinite number of other moments of the same kind, when death is as natural as life, and both of them happen to us in the same manner without our feeling them, without our being able to appreciate them?

"Question physicians and ministers of the Church, who are accustomed to observe the movements of the dying and to listen to their last expressions of feeling. They will all agree in saying that except in the case of a very small number of acute illnesses, where the agitation caused by convulsive movements seems to indicate the sufferings of the patient, death comes to us quietly, calmly, and painlessly. And even the terrible agonies to which I have referred cause more fear to the onlooker than torment to the invalid. Time and time again we hear of persons who have been at this last extremity but who have retained no recollection of what has happened or of what they have felt! As far as they themselves are concerned they have really ceased to exist during that period, for they are obliged to erase from the total number of their days those which they have spent in this condition and of which they have preserved no recollection.

"Most of us, then, die without knowing it. And among the few who preserve their intelligence unto the last, there is scarcely one who does not at the

194

same time preserve some hope and delude himself into believing that he will return to life. For the good of man, Nature has given more strength to this sentiment than to reason. An invalid whose illness is incurable, who can judge of his state by frequent and familiar examples, who is warned of it by the anxious gestures of his family, by the weeping of his friends, by the bearing of the doctors, is none the more convinced that his last hour has struck. Our interest in the matter is so great that we refer it to no other judgement than our own. We have no faith in the opinions of others. We regard them as ill-founded alarms. Whatever we may feel and think, we reflect and reason only for our own good. Everything else may die, but hope lives on.

"Cast your eyes on an invalid who has told you a hundred times that he thinks he is desperately ill, that he is perfectly sure that he cannot recover, that he is on the point of death; note his change of expression when, either through zeal or indiscretion, someone tells him that his end is really near. You will see him start like one to whom some unexpected news has been announced. This invalid, then, does not believe what he says about himself; he is not at all convinced that he must die. He is only a little doubtful, a little anxious, about his state of health. But he fears much less than he hopes. And were we not to awake his fears by the tearful care and the lugubrious accoutrements that announce the approach of death, he would never see it come."

* * *

o 2

Obliviousness or hope—these, then, are the great palliatives for death. It would be impossible to stretch optimism further than Buffon does in the passage quoted. How beautifully peaceful it would be if things were really as he represents them!

But there is still room for doubt. Firstly, is it true that "terrible agonies" are so rare? I freely confess that if my agony were conscious, if I were to see myself die, that would be enough to reopen the door to suffering, possibly to despair. And even if the agony is peaceful outwardly, from the observer's point of view, who knows what is happening within the soul of the person who is dying? Perhaps he suffers mental torture worse than the worst physical convulsions. Even supposing there is unconsciousness so long as the human make-up subsists, so long as the patient is still breathing, how about the actual 'passing', the moment when what is known as the 'cessation of life'—the detaching or tearing—takes place? Is it true that unconsciousness still persists or is a new form of consciousness awakened? No one who has escaped from death can give us information on the subject because he has not experienced it.

The reasonings of the naturalist and materialist philosophers do not succeed, then, in extirpating all our doubts. Moreover, we call to mind the cry of alarm uttered by Seneca: "By what eloquence, by what force of genius, can you undermine this universal consent to fear, this conviction of the whole human race which steadfastly opposes you?"

It is only too true: there is a universal consent to

fear, not exactly the fear of death itself but of the subject of death.

At the mere picture of it, at the mere suspicion of it, the vital instinct revolts in horror, and not only in the case of man but also of the beasts. They feel it to be a menace, a mysterious enemy that will overcome them in the end, or at any rate a diminution of their being and their strength, a serious attack on their ability to live. They behave in the presence of death as they would in the presence of a lion: their hair bristles with terror and they run away to hide themselves. When a cat feels the approach of death it quits the dwelling to which it is so attached and goes a considerable distance away to die in some retreat that it thinks to be impenetrable. It seems to be fleeing from an unseen enemy whose breath it feels at its back. Sometimes men behave in like manner. I know of old men who are still robust, but, sensing the threat of apoplexy, force themselves to take long walks, to make fatiguing journeys, to be continually shifting their abode, as though death were on their heels, as though they were trying to run away from it, or at any rate to keep it at a distance. On scenting carrion a horse will rear or shy. The ox snorts at the smell of blood or on nearing the slaughter-house. It is not the simple, instinctive reaction in the face of danger, since the danger does not exist—as yet; it is the fear of diminution, of something that is ominous or fatal for them. I remember an occasion when I fell down near one of my cats and remained stretched out on the floor, unable to move. The animal was first of all frightened by the noise I had made in falling, then, seeing that I did not stir, it approached me with hesitating little steps, and finally it stood quite still in an attitude of terror. It was very much like a human being in the presence of a corpse.

* * *

The vital instinct boggles at the very idea of death, that is, of an enemy that menaces our very being. And it revolts at the thought of what death robs us of; it is a diminution, not only of our being but of everything that touches our being, everything that augments our feeling of power, everything that enhances the value of life. Those who are not sufficiently detached from the blessings or the pleasures of this world, or who, not disdaining to enjoy them, have been unable to despise them—these persons suffer cruelly from the rending effect of the separation. They are fortunate if by dint of reason they eventually become resigned. But what a catastrophe and what suffering for those who will not accept their fate! . . . Ah! So much the worse for those who have given their heart to what is not eternal! I often hear this said of one recently deceased, as though it were a tribute: "He was so much in love with life!" Unhappy man! How he must have suffered in seeing it elude his grasp!

I am always thinking of the last illness of Cardinal Mazarin. He was a great collector, a great lover of works of art, and was strongly attracted by a life of pomp and splendour. In ecclesiastical language, he had attached his heart to 'idols', that is to say, to the contour of a statue, to the form or the texture of a vase, to the colour or the varnish of a painting. And suddenly he had to detach himself from all these things, without which life was nothing but a desert! . . . The young Brienne, in his *Mémoires*, represents him on the day before he died, paying a last visit to his picture-gallery, leaning on his stick and shuffling along in his bedroom slippers. Before this or that rare tapestry or priceless object he would stop and sigh: "To think that all this must be left!" . . . I think also of another cardinal, this time a contemporary of our own, who began life in humble circumstances and was brought up amid rough if not actually indigent conditions. He was just a little dazzled by the honours and the life of ease and dignity that fell to his lot, and he thoroughly enjoyed living in a comfortable mansion and having at his disposal all its various amenities. On leaving it to undergo an operation, from which, no doubt, he feared he would not return, he stopped for a moment to take a farewell glance at the dwelling which had given him so much pleasure. "This is a nice way," said he, "to have to leave one's home!"

These sad words, concealed, perhaps, a sore distress of mind. I tremble to think that this Prince of the Church was not sufficiently detached from pleasure, albeit of a modest kind. And even if he were—and I should like to think so—he could not prevent that cruel turn of the wheel which by involving certain separations wrings the heart.

Finally I turn to consider my own case. Though I cherish the belief that I am quite detached, I may be less so than the cardinal. There are times when the mental picture of certain events, the sensation of certain joys or emotions, take shape again with such force, with such fascinating charm, that it plunges us into gloom to think that they will never return, that they are lost for ever. I feel that on such and such an occasion I attained the zenith of my life. My heart is bound up with these intoxicating, exalting things, and now they are nothing but a mirage. No matter, I give them my heart! These are my only loves, these are my only regrets. . . . We know very well that it is foolish, but we suffer no less cruelly for knowing it. . . .

Even believers who await the delights of the beatific vision in an ecstasy of hope, who are perfectly certain that the next world will be infinitely more beautiful than this, even they are unable to overcome a feeling of regret at having to part with the humble things they have loved on this earth. I confess that I can never read certain passages from my friend Emile Baumann's *Trois Villes Saintes* without emotion and a bitter, homesick feeling. After displaying before our eyes the delights of Paradise he reverts to his native land and bids it this unforgettably sweet and melancholy farewell: "Lord, how can I love your new skies and new country, when this one here is so beautiful that it cuts me to the heart to tear myself away from it? You who have made the wind and the sea, the dawn and the night, let me weep now for this world to which

You yourself came down, for the sweetness of the green leaves, for the ox and the ass of your crib, for the children who jump on their parents' and grand-parents' knees, for the house where we were born!"

Even supposing we credit the believer, or the philosopher, with a complete detachment, a renunciation and a constancy that enable him to contemplate the most fearful possibilities with perfect equanimity, even then he would not be completely proof against the surprises that his instinct might have in store for him. We imagine we have reached the *templa serena* of wisdom or religious asceticism and then we suddenly find ourselves thrown out of them by some inexplicable disturbance. We are attacked by obscure forces. A fit of panic, a sudden assault by the old ancestral terrors rising up from the uttermost depths of our being, lay us low and scatter to right and left the flimsy shelters of our reason. We lose our heads, we shiver and shake, or our heart and our soul are stricken with gloom: death is once again a bugbear and a torture.

* * *

But note that this terror and this desolation are not death itself, they are not death *in actu ;* they are only the apprehension of it, a purely subjective state that can be overcome. Note, too, that these mental depressions usually occur when the vital sense is at an ebb, when the organism has been attacked, that is to say they are the concomitants of a state of physical depression. On such occasions the instinct sounds the alarm, fights madly, and becomes unhinged. I have noticed that I am most terrified by death when I am passing through a crisis or when I am beset by some physiological disturbance, for example when an illness is at its height or during the indeterminate phase preceding convalescence. The death of others never upsets me so much when I am in good health as when I feel that I too am threatened, that is to say when I am seriously ill. Then I have to submit, without resistance, without reaction, to all the turbulent motions of the instinct.

On the other hand, when we are very much alive, how little we care about death! We feel ourselves to be borne along irresistibly by the surge of life. We are like the swimmer in the open sea, a mere speck in the boundless ocean, but one who feels himself to be supported by all the forces of the colossal element. At such uplifting moments, when we imagine we are masters of ourselves and of the universe, how strong we are in the face of death, how we despise it! It reminds me of Bossuet's words: "We all know that we have to die, but we don't believe it." We believe it well enough, but we snap our fingers at it. All-powerful life upholds us and thus we have the strength to sustain the shock of the most depressing thoughts and to contemplate with calm the prospect of the most frightful possibilities. I remember an occasion when I was leaving home to undergo an operation which might easily have proved fatal. I was perfectly cheerful, and quite resigned never to see my home again. In fact, I was almost delighted at the prospect. And why? It was because I was not so ill as I must have imagined myself to be. Life was still supporting me securely. My animal instinct was fortifying me at the moment when my imagination was taking fright, and its assurance outweighed all my fears. Those who have been condemned to death are in the same case. Read the reports of executions: most of the victims bear up well, even without the consolation that Dostoievsky had when he was sentenced to be shot, the consolation of telling themselves that they are about to die like martyrs for a cause that must promote the welfare of the human race. It is their vital instinct alone that upholds them.

Hugo's *Le Dernier Jour d'un Condamné* is a gloomy nightmare belied by everyday experience. Among innumerable examples I recall that of a young engineer from Lorraine who, at the beginning of the last war, was sentenced by the Germans to be shot for refusing to give them information about the French defences. He assured me that he spent the days and nights preceding the execution with the utmost tranquillity. Having put his affairs in order and cleared his conscience with the assistance of a priest, he was ready to devote what time remained to reading and reflection. Like Dostoievsky, he was pardoned at the last moment by the Emperor. The first effect of the reprieve was to throw him into a state of complete bewilderment. He was ready to die, he had adjusted himself to the situation, and the unexpected news had upset everything again. It was only afterwards that he rejoiced. . . .

I have been in danger of death myself on more than one occasion, and I subsequently realized that at the critical moment my attention was wholly taken up in parrying the blows or in disposing myself so as to suffer the least possible hurt. At such moments as these we are completely in the power of our instinct, and our instinct is wholly occupied with the business of self-protection. Even when there is time for reflection, the mind, too, swayed as it is by the instinct, thinks of nothing but self-protection. Once when I was on a steamer caught in a cyclone I lay in my bunk watching enormous waves dashing against the porthole. I had no other thought but as to how I could meet my death in the least unpleasant manner. I weighed the pros and the cons: should I stay where I was, and be suffocated in my bunk by the invading mass of water, or run up on deck and amid the panic and the shrieks of despair throw myself into the sea, with the probability of never leaving it, or spend hours of agonizing suspense in a lifeboat? Once I had made up my mind I was comparatively calm: the vital instinct was still strong within me; this, and hope, buoyed me up. . . . I remember another occasion, when I was thrown from my horse. It had bolted with me, and I was certain I should fall and very likely break my neck, but all I thought of was how I could manage to land in the least dangerous position. . . .

Even those persons who in virtue of their vocation

have trained themselves to think of death—I mean the clergy and philosophers—even they will tell you that the last thing they will think of in an emergency is death. Like the simplest human being they are wholly absorbed by the instinct of self-preservation. An eminent prelate, a colleague of mine at the Institut de France, who was an out-and-out Parisian, having lived in the capital all his life, told us that one day he had slipped and fallen in a busy thoroughfare and found himself in imminent danger of being run over by a motor-bus. This pious man, finding himself within an ace of death, thought only of escaping it, and all he could say to himself was: "I thought I had a more Parisian foot than that!" If he had stayed where he was, that would have been his penultimate thought. . . .

We see, then, that so long as we are fully alive we are not afraid of death. I mean to say that when we are in a state of vital integrity the danger of immediate death does not disturb us. For this reason sudden death is probably the most merciful. But we must not rely too firmly on this triumphant reaction of the vital instinct, since, as we have said before, it is only too prone to fail us at the critical moment. Among those who have been condemned to death some indeed accept their fate and can control themselves bravely to the end, but others, such as the Dubarry, for instance, and certain criminals of a lower order, break down and struggle pitiably. Such deaths as these must be the most terrible of all, and the most degrading. . . . But who can answer for his nerves—or even his will, if it is not sustained by something stronger than itself? When human nature is thrown out of joint by an imminent danger, a mere nothing—a chance gesture, a sudden thought, a song, a word—may send us into convulsions. . . . When, during that cyclone, I lay in my bunk thinking of the safest way of escaping a lingering death, I was not yet in the actual presence of death. I wonder what would have happened to my resolutions if I had seen the porthole shattered by a wave, and a huge torrent of water pour into the cabin?

* * *

The vital instinct, then, is not reliable. By a contradiction inherent in human nature, the same force that sustains us against death in some circumstances may betray us in others.

Consequently it is well to strengthen it, to fortify it, against its own infirmities, and the only means we have at our disposal for effecting this is reason. Can it succeed in its task? If it can, up to what point?

CHAPTER IV

REASON AND DEATH

DEATH may be nothing to the physiologist, or the naturalist, or primitive man; to them it may be just an ordinary accident, a natural phenomenon like any other, but for most of us it is a serious matter, in fact *the* matter. For what, at rock bottom, is our prime concern? Living. And death appears to be the negation of this desire of ours which is the very essence of our being. It is the great obstacle, the incomprehensible obstacle. Hence its supreme importance. Hence also the fact that even those races which submit to it with the greatest ease or apparent indifference, even they take care to devote to it very special rites. They realize that death is something awe-inspiring, that it is a fact quite different from other facts, with a significance all its own. The rites of death are more elaborate, more impressive, than those of birth. One is almost tempted to say that for most people death is of more importance than birth. For birth is a normal event, whereas death seems to be something abnormal, *something that ought not to be*, that upsets the established order of things.

This doubtless is the reason why all races, at all times, have surrounded death with such ceremonial. Dirges, wakes, funeral games, burial rites, are clear evidence of the exceptional significance man attaches to death. On this point reason and instinct are in accord, but despite our instinctive terror, reason has always striven to show that, however alarming it may appear, death is really nothing to be frightened of.

* * *

Reason tells us that the objects of our fears may be defined as annihilation, separation from, and loss of, goods and persons who are dear to us, horror of the 'passing', and uncertainty about our future state.

We will not quote any of the philosophic clichés, ancient or modern, about the necessity of man's coming to an end, and the advantages of resigning ourselves to our fate: everything, we are told, has to end some time; everything in Nature dies. But it is precisely from this ending that the average man recoils. We are quite willing for everything to die—with the exception of ourselves. The sole consideration capable of moderating this frantic desire to live is that under present conditions eternal living would be wearisome beyond endurance and that, willy-nilly, we should be compelled to long for death to release us from a life that is worse than death itself. Since Lucretius, and even before, naturalist philosophers have been saying to mankind: "What are you afraid of? When you are annihilated you will cease to suffer. It will be your release. It will be deep, untroubled, everlasting peace!"

We frankly admit, however, that the prospect of an eternal rest of which we shall be utterly unconscious and which, therefore, we shall not appreciate, hardly reconciles us to the thought of death. The unpleasant part of the business still remains: the necessity of coming to an end, and that perhaps in suffering or despair.

The non-materialist philosophers inform us: "On the hypothesis of survival after death, annihilation is only apparent: Death is only a change of plane, the passing to another life, to the definitive and true life." If we leave on one side the religions that affirm this theory and demand our faith, there is no positive proof of it. Such an affirmation on the part of reason only would be hazardous. The philosophers who uphold it are reduced to bringing forward against the annihilation theory this very need of living which is continually frustrated and, so to speak, denied, by death. And what right has one to affirm that this frantic desire to live can be finally triumphant *in the individual?* Certainly it triumphs in Nature, in the myriad forms of life that are born and perish, but does it do so in the individual? . . . We are forced back on the old argument of finality: from the fact that a thing tends to act, that is, it tends towards a certain end, therefore the end must inevitably be attained. This was the view adopted finally by Barrès, as we see from the following reflections found among his private papers:

"What must be—what my intelligence demands —is a future life—either of reward or punishment— or, more simply, *something that gives a meaning to suffering*. My intelligence foresees that eventually our ten miles of atmosphere will be reduced, that the earth will cease to move (no matter after what lapse of time—time does not exist), and that therefore the day will come when it will be as if we had never existed. My intelligence refuses to accept this. It demands that there should be something else besides this void.

"But kindly note that it is not a question of some sentimental need, of a desire to be reunited in another world with those who are dear to us here. No, I mean that my intelligence is so made that it cannot admit that all this is as it is and that it is all a void. My intelligence needs, desires, demands, something in addition, and just as Le Verrier believes that a star will appear at the end of his telescope, so I believe in another life." [1]

In other words, Barrès, like every other adherent of the non-materialist opinion, cannot admit that an act, once commenced, may fail to attain its end; thought is a commencement which assumes its accomplishment, otherwise it would be an absurdity. Pain must have a meaning or an object, otherwise it would be an incomprehensible monstrosity. . . . But what a frail argument this is! So far as reason goes, an incomprehensible monstrosity is perfectly admissible. Thought can perfectly well continue and subsist outside the individual, in a collective form; the world's thought, if not the individual's, may be eternal. Besides, the ego is not the measure of things. Why should the "needs" of our intellect impose themselves on the universe? If Le Verrier's hypothesis is plausible it is because the star has come, or

[1] *Cf.* "Mes Cahiers: Fragments sur la Religion," in the *Revue Universelle* of May 15th, 1933.

will come, to confirm it, whereas, from the point of view of reason pure and simple, nothing confirms the hypothesis of the future life. As Amiel says, "A wish is not a proof."

* * *

Reason alone, then, can furnish us with proofs, neither of the total annihilation of the individual, nor of his future life. The most it can give us are likely presumptions, but those are not sufficient to calm our fears.

But supposing that these hypotheses were proved, would reason be any more capable of consoling us for the separation brought about by either annihilation or an entry into another life? To be separated from our belongings and those that are dear to us— ever since the world has been the world, this has been one of death's most cruel torments. Ever since man has been in existence and has suffered, he has groaned at the thought that death not only robs him of everything to which he is attached but that even his least enjoyments are darkened by its shadow. Death spoils everything, it gives everything the taste of ashes. And the pain of separation is the most inconsolable of all. . . .

Philosophers maintain the opposite view, that the thought of death is a stimulant, or at least a season-ing, for pleasure. "In order to enjoy life," says Seneca, "we must be ever ready to quit it." But the inherent miseries of life are more effective than any exhortation in detaching us from pleasure, which in any case is always precarious and incomplete. Satiation, the weariness of living, the *tædium vitæ*, the realization of the incorrigible wickedness, the incurable baseness of mankind, the feeling of the uselessness of striving, and the conviction that, in the words of the Scriptures, "the nations consume themselves in fire"—all this facilitates detachment and the final separation.

Is it more difficult to renounce our affections? Let us remember that everlasting unions are hardly part of this world, that human love is doomed to engender satiation, indifference, and finally, enmity, that even friendship is not secure from misunderstandings, disappointments, quarrels, intrigues, and lassitude resulting from monotony. . . . I turn my thoughts to my friends who have recently died. I think of them with regret, with sorrow. I had, and I still have, a great affection for them. But, if I am to be sincere with myself, I must admit that my suffering is caused less by their separation from me than by the shock of their death. The thought that they have been so brutally taken out of my life, by an accident that threatens to abolish me before long, the thought that they might never have existed so far as I am concerned—that is what insults me and afflicts me, that is the true significance of my pain. It is the cruel, humiliating proof, by means of an event that affects me personally, of the insignificance of a human life. . . .

An acquaintance of mine expresses his view on the matter thus: "The last thing to make me believe in, or look forward to, a future life is the 'final reunion', the theme on which Loti composed so

many melancholy or despairing variations. To him
it was either an impossibility or a hopeless longing.
Well, I've no desire at all in this direction. I'm not
anxious to renew my acquaintance with most of the
human beings I have met. The idea of an everlasting
tête-à-tête with any one of them would put me off
Paradise for ever. As for those I was fond of, if I do
look forward to seeing them again, it is solely in
God. It is God alone I want!"

* * *

Some separations, if not more painful than sentimental ones, seem at least to us to be more unjustifi-
able and more incomprehensible. I mean those
which, after they have robbed us of our pleasures
and our affections, deprive us of our appetite for
knowledge and creation, which put a sudden stop to
some important work already undertaken, which
shatter our aspiration for terrestrial glory and
immortality. Those were our most noble, our most
lofty, ambitions; surely they ought to be respected!
To see them thwarted and jeered at like all the
others rends our heart more cruelly than anything.

But the reason holds in reserve a goodly selection
of maxims wherewith we may console ourselves.
What is the use of anything that is not eternal?
What is our wretched desire for knowledge compared with the mystery that oppresses us on every
side? It is surely the most ridiculous of ambitions.
After all said and done, what is human glory, the
reputation of a poet, or a statesman, or a soldier? A
thousand years from now, who will remember

Napoleon, Virgil, or Homer? For all we know, our whole civilization may be on the brink of ruin.

No one has surpassed Chateaubriand in expressing this utter disillusionment, this detachment from everything that is not eternal, but this does not prevent a cunning and ineradicable vanity from insinuating itself below his deep-rooted wisdom. It is easy enough to accuse of vanity a man who was not only a great Christian but also a great writer. It is useless for him to repeat *ad nauseam* that "everything in this world ends in a coffin"; it does not alter the fact that he was proud of being the author of *Atala* and *Les Martyrs*, and prouder still, perhaps, of having been an ambassador, a peer of the realm, a Minister for Foreign Affairs, and a counsellor of kings. And it is equally certain that he was just as sincere—perhaps more so—in despising all the titles and honours of his double career. Just as Louis XIV considered that humility was a virtue proper to kings, Chateaubriand was convinced that it was proper to those who have experienced renown.

The humility which consists in smashing everything, in trampling everything under foot, after achieving all one's ambitions, is possibly the last revenge of pride. Even supposing the humility is perfect, it must be painful underneath the surface. Like sensual pleasure, sacrifice has an after-taste that all the approval of conscience and reason is powerless to remove.

* * *

Up to a certain point wisdom can console us for the painful element in every kind of separation. Can it fortify us even more effectively against the horror of the 'passing'?

Once more we are told what we have already heard from Buffon: "Don't be frightened! Death is sweet. Death is absolutely painless. We die as we are born—without realizing it." Further, we are assured that the majority of those about to die are devoid of fear. Among innumerable other cases we are asked to consider that of Laënnec,[1] who, two hours before his death—which he knew to be imminent—took off his rings and laid them on the table by his bed. On being asked why he did so, he replied: "Someone will have to do it for me soon, and I should like to save him such a painful duty."

That is tantamount to heroism. Also, the man in question was one of the *élite;* but we are told that the same attitude is evinced by the most ordinary of mortals. The evidence that follows comes from the most varied sources. An English member of parliament states: "Having been the parliamentary representative for the University of Edinburgh for seventeen years, I have naturally been in contact with some of the most eminent physicians in the British Isles. I have put this question to nearly all of them: 'Have you ever, in the course of your experience, known a patient to be afraid of death?' With possibly two exceptions they all answered in the negative."

One of the best-known physicians in London is of much the same opinion. When he was studying at

---

[1] René Laënnec (1781–1826), the famous French physician who discovered and popularized the auscultation test.

Guy's he arranged with the sister in charge of the wards where he was working to let him know whenever a patient was on the point of death. "I wanted," he said, "apart from my usual duties, to obtain some knowledge of the facts that prelude death." And this is the information he obtained: "I shall never tire of saying this, because I am convinced that it is not only comforting but true, although it is contrary to general belief. Death does not inspire the patient with fear. . . . There is nothing terrifying about death for the person who is dying. The veil between the two worlds is nothing more than a cloud through which we pass without being aware of it."

Here is the evidence of another doctor:

"I have taken careful notes on about five hundred fatal cases, giving special attention to the manner of death and the sensations of the dying. Ninety underwent physical suffering, or anxiety of some kind or another; eleven displayed mental apprehension; two, definite terror; one, spiritual exaltation ; and one, bitter remorse. The great majority betrayed no feelings at all, in any direction. They no more felt their death than they had felt their birth; they just dropped off into a sleep that had no end."

Even in the worst type of accident, it is claimed, the dying person either has no knowledge of his sufferings or he passes through curious states of well-being. A man who narrowly escaped death by drowning thus analyses the sensations he experienced before losing consciousness entirely: "I heard bells ringing in the distance, and other pleasant little sounds struck upon my ears. After that I was regaled with pleasant visions. All the colours of the rainbow danced before my eyes and, mingling together, formed all kinds of curious patterns. I had no suffering whatever, and I had no anxiety about what was going to happen next. What I saw, delighted me. Everything was calm and airy and seemed to be moved by some invisible force. I felt as though I were looking into a mirror where I saw the most beautiful things the imagination could conceive. Towards the end, the beauty of everything increased. There was not a single discordant sound, only the sweetest, the most delicious, music. I seemed to have been transported into a region flooded with brilliant but soothing light."

Among a score of similar cases there is one of a hunter who was struck down by a tiger and averred that he felt no pain at all while the beast was devouring the whole length of his arm, from hand to shoulder. "The man experienced not the slightest feeling of fear, and the pain was negligible. He felt some pain when the animal's fangs were piercing his hand, but he felt nothing *while his arm was being masticated*." [1]

Painless mastication of the arm sounds incredible and faintly comic: so does the drowning man who before losing consciousness attends a concert and watches a succession of delightful pictures. How much credit is to be given to these analyses made after the event? To have any value, the sensations

[1] This and the foregoing instances are taken from Henry de Varigny's *La Mort et le Sentiment*.

ought to be analysed at the time. Furthermore, is it possible to express such extraordinary sensations in ordinary language? Think of the difficulty experienced by mystics when they try to describe analogous situations, or even by us when we try to describe our dreams. However undramatic the accident may have been, the victim of it inevitably yields to the temptation of making it dramatic. The subject who is observed or questioned by a psychiatrist always acts more or less in conformity with the latter's preconceived suggestions or ideas.

But even on the supposition that all these cases have been accurately observed, it will be noted that in these dreary statistics the number of painful deaths is sufficiently large to revive or sustain our fears. Moreover, in the case of a peaceful death, or rather one which shows every sign of being peaceful, who knows what is happening behind those closed eyes and mouth, behind that brow which is already as pale and cold as marble? That peaceful exterior may be deceptive; still more so when the patient shows every sign of suffering: for the suffering may be not only physical but mental. Confirmed optimists—those who believe in the universal benignity of death—base their belief on the testimony of those who have been in its clutches and have escaped it. These latter assure us that they have either felt nothing at all or have experienced only agreeable sensations. "Another second or two," they declare, "and without knowing it I should have passed into complete unconsciousness." We hear this kind of talk especially from those who have undergone the slow poisoning of gas. . . . But they were still alive when they sank into their torpor. Death has not yet done its work. All that they had known was the state preliminary to death itself, the state preceding the 'passing'. How are we to know what happens during this last phase, when the vital functions definitely cease? None of those who have experienced it have lived to tell the tale.

On this point reason cannot give us any absolute assurance. It is by no means proven that the passing takes place without our being aware of it or suffering any pain.

* * *

Let us consider the matter in its worst possible light. Let us suppose that the sufferings of the death-agony and the 'passing' are real and of frequent occurrence. Many philosophies and religions will give us for answer: We must resign ourselves gladly to these sufferings and trials because they enable us to attain to a higher kind of life. Death is the means of entering eternity, which must be a state of happiness for the wise and dutiful. *"Dies iste quem tanquam extremum reformidas æterni natalis est.—*That day which you dread as though it were your last is in reality your birthday in eternity."

Eternity is a terrifying thought! How and with what are we to form such a conception? How dare we presume that eternity is everlasting happiness or the peace of absolute annihilation? Both hypotheses are equally indemonstrable. Only religious faith can assure us that eternity may be everlasting happiness. It proclaims that God is infinitely kind, but it proclaims also that His justice is terrible. While awaiting it, therefore, we must tremble. Freethinkers congratulate believers unnecessarily when they say to them: "How lucky you are to have the faith! For you death is nothing but the entry into a life of happiness."

Unfortunately, this is far from being certain. How many sermons have been preached on "the few that are chosen"! This, no doubt, is why men of faith die in fear and trembling, while miscreants die with perfect equanimity.

No philosophy can guarantee eternal rest to the latter; it cannot justify their tranquillity with any irrefutable reason. It is no use our giving our attention to the jumble of philosophic, 'scientific', theosophic, esoteric, or even spiritualistic, opinions on what will happen to us after death. They lead us nowhere, and provide us with nothing but illusions. Let us hold fast rather to the most prudent rationalistic presumption: that death is the means of entry into eternity.

How does a Stoic like Seneca conceive this entry? He conceives it as a vanishing into the divine substance. Our personality will be left behind on the threshold. The present forms of our consciousness, all that makes us individuals, are inadmissible by the Eternal and the Absolute. Well, our personality, our ego, is what we cling to most. This entry into eternity would be just as much death as ever— whatever fine promises may be made to us—the death of the being that we are! And that is what we fear the most.

And yet—this personality—we are not at all certain as to what it is. We dare not plumb the mystery too deeply. As Chateaubriand said: "We spend our whole life asking ourselves the question: 'Who are you?' and we never know the answer."

* * *

The most ingenious reasoning, the most seductive prospects for the future, will never succeed in calming completely the panics of the instinct. Even reason cannot free itself from all its doubts concerning death. The most it can do is to prepare us for what cannot be avoided.

For thousands of years the schools of philosophy and the various religions have been warning us that life must be nothing but a preparation for death. "Have it always in your mind," says Seneca, "so that you will never fear it!" This counsel is echoed by Montaigne in his famous lines: "Let nothing be so often in our thoughts as death! Let us bring it before our imagination at every moment and in every shape and form. At the stumbling of a horse, at the falling of a tile, at the slightest prick of a pin, let the thought immediately recur to us: 'Well? And what if it had been death itself?"

A little further on, the same author says with a rather disconcerting turn of thought: "I hope that death will find me planting cabbages, *quite unconcerned with it.*"

But the contradiction is only an apparent one. Both attitudes depend on our temperament and frame of mind. The same man can, at one moment, make it his duty to think of death, and at another, not to think of it. Both attitudes are equally natural, both can be justified by philosophic reasoning. There are some who are always thinking of it, and there are others who, on principle and for reasons of mental hygiene, refuse to think of it at all. Goethe's maxim, for instance, was: "Away with death! Let us set our faces to the future!" If we want to act, we shun the thought of death, if not actually scoff at it. This perpetual meditation on death recommended by philosophers and priests—is there not a risk of its enervating us and making us afraid of life, of making us sink into a dull indifference? For, once again, what are we in search of, what do we desire? We desire to live. We tend towards a more intense, a higher, life. Are we setting about the accomplishment of this desire in the right way by despising this life here, which is the necessary preliminary to the next—if there is a next? Our present life is the basis of everything. Let us begin by living well, then, and all the rest will be added unto us.

Actually the two tendencies are perfectly reconcilable. We can live well, we can be intensely active, while making our life a meditation on death. Even the mystics who were most detached from the world never ceased to carry out this rule. Those who have had the gift of interior living to an extraordinary degree have also been great realists. St. Teresa travelled the length and breadth of Spain in order to found convents, to organize institutions, to importune generous donors, to provide for the material needs of her religious. It is one of the great rules of Christian morals : mortification, renunciation, are not enough; we must act, as much as we can, to our dying breath. Bourdaloue attached great importance to this consideration, notably in his *Instructions à une Personne de Qualité*. "Take care lest the detachment from the world caused by the thought of death turn into indifference and possibly into disgust for the things to which God wishes you to apply yourself and which are the duties allotted you by Providence. By dint of contemplating death, by seeing it so near you, you may lapse into distaste and indifference for everything in the world, with the result that you will slacken even in your duties, because you will cease to find anything in the world that is worth the trouble of giving it your affection."

Wisdom, therefore, counsels us not to cease from action, while estimating this life and our actions at their true value. The important point is to familiarize ourselves with the idea of death and to fortify ourselves against its dispiriting aspects. Can we rely on this preparation serving us in good stead at the final issue? We cannot be absolutely sure. We may be deserted by our strength of mind; our physical weakness may hand us over to the ragings of our instinct. But this preparation is to take effect not so much at the final moment as here and now. It is now, when we are in good health, that it is to have its salutary effect, by freeing us from vain terrors, by subduing the revolts of the instinct and the disturbances of the mind.

As we have seen, there is every likelihood that death may be gentle at the end. If it is not, it may indeed be terrible. The believer can at least hope for supernatural strengthening and succour at the last. And the Apostle assures him that he will not be tempted, that is to say, tried beyond his strength.

CHAPTER V

THE SIMPLE TRUTH

W E have not advanced a single step towards the solution of the problem; we have simply taken up a certain attitude towards the 'passing.' And we feel more or less intensely, according to our temperament, that this 'passing' is of capital importance for our future life. On this point, too, priests and philosophers are in accord. We recall the solemn warning of the Abbé de Rancé, the great reformer of the Trappists: "We die once only. The mistakes we make in our first life cannot be repaired in our second. *Whatever we are at the moment when we die, we shall be for always.*" The religions of India, on the contrary, maintain that we die more than once, but, with Schopenhauer, they hold that our reincarnations or rebirths depend on the dispositions we were in when we died. Hence the really tragic importance of the 'passing'; hence our inability to resign ourselves to knowing nothing of the matter. Unwearyingly our thoughts prowl round and round the impenetrable abyss.

Anxiously we bend over to watch the agonies of the dying. . . .

* * *

The mask of death tells us nothing. Externally it seems to stir our curiosity in order the better to mislead it. So far as my brief personal experience is concerned, the bodies and faces of the dead present to me two general aspects or expressions.

In the one case they present an appearance of profound peace, of almost joyous serenity. The dead person seems to be absorbed in the enjoyment of the beatitude that follows acute suffering, or physical and mental crises; he seems to be wrapped in a delicious slumber—to be still alive. Sometimes—it may be merely my imagination—the flesh seems to be utterly devoid of life, as inert as marble or bronze, but touched by the reflection of some indeterminable joy, a kind of light, that the soul has left behind it at the moment of departure.

In the other case they present the lamentable appearance of something used and done with: a dead branch lying by the side of a field, a stone which, from a distance, looks like a statue of a human being, but which has no eyes, or mouth, or face, and seems to be the very negation of life. This aspect is the most depressing. One would think that the corpse had never been inhabited by a soul. In any case, it is finished now for good and all; there is no connection between that *thing* and us. And the thought that that nothingness was once like us appals us.

* * *

How are we to delve into the depths of souls? How are we to guess at what is happening in the souls of the dying, who, before breathing their last—or long previously, in many cases—have been deprived of all means of communicating with us?

It cannot be too often reiterated that the tales told by those who have been on the point of death must be regarded with the greatest circumspection. Their imagination leads them astray, even against their will. Moreover, it is impossible for them to express in ordinary language the experiences they have actually undergone. There is one feature, however, common to the accounts given by those who have narrowly escaped death and to the delirium of the dying: the extraordinary, monstrous, activity of the imagination. People who have been on the verge of death by drowning, hanging, or asphyxiation claim to have seen a succession of marvellous pictures, including astonishing landscapes, during the lucid periods that precede or follow those of complete unconsciousness. And merely to hear the words let fall by the dying in their delirium is sufficient to convince us that the scenes they are witnessing are just as real to them as those of normal life.

In dreams also and in hypnotic states resulting from accidents or certain pathological conditions, the imagination seems to be endowed with a force that in some cases borders, as it were, on genius. We have all seen in our dreams landscapes and buildings of which we had no conception—which might be said to have come to us from another world. Sometimes these visions are so clear that they leave a distinct impression on the memory and we are able to describe them with as much vividness and detail as though we had seen them in our waking moments. They are frequently magnificent or prodigious, but they are characterized by a certain illogicality and absurdity. At other times they seem to have all the solid and rational characteristics of reality. And on waking, the dreamer— even if he has a professional knowledge of form—is amazed at what his imagination could create. But I fear that this quasi-genial activity of the imagination is totally illusory. Is it not more or less analogous to television? During the periods of hypnosis brought about by accidents or morbid conditions—and, in a lesser degree, in a dream—may not the imagination be likened to a sensitive plate that registers automatically shapes and colours that come from a great distance and have been carried to the subject's sensibility by unknown paths?

This is pure hypothesis, but whatever the truth of the matter be, these cases are, if not actually related, at least comparable with those of the mystics, who, during their meditations, ecstasies, or raptures, are aware of feelings or matters of which they had no previous idea—with this difference, however, that the mystic attributes a far greater reality to this kind of experience than to those of normal life, whereas those who have been dreaming or delirious consider their experiences to be purely illusory or absurd.

What is certain is that the mystic, when in a state that he considers to be as near to death as possible, is aware of things that are otherwise totally unknown to him. Further, he is convinced that he has been brought into a world the reality of which eclipses that of the world to which he is accustomed. How are these assertions to be verified? What is certain is that the mystic passes through conditions that are strangely similar to death. In her autobiography,[1] which is a collection of observations made at the time with the most scrupulous exactness, St. Teresa affirms this in the most definite manner. At the same time she gives us reason for supposing that during her meditations as well as during her ecstasies or raptures—that is to say in conditions bordering on death—a new kind of consciousness takes the place of the individual consciousness, which is totally submerged.

"During raptures," says the saint, "the soul does not seem to animate the body, the natural heat of which is perceptibly lessened; the coldness increases. . . . Sometimes my pulse ceases, as it were, to beat at all—so the sisters say, who sometimes approach me, and who now understand the matter better— my bones are racked, and my hands become so rigid, that I cannot always join them. Even on the following day I have a pain in my wrists, and over my whole body, as if my bones were out of joint." In her *Moradas*, too, she devotes considerable attention to these external phenomena. "Almost as soon as I have entered into a rapture I cease to breathe, and although sometimes I may retain the use of my other senses for a moment I cannot utter a single word. Frequently, however, I lose control of all my

[1] The translation of the extracts that follow is in part that made by David Lewis (2nd ed.; 1888). TR.

senses simultaneously. My hands and my whole body become so cold that my soul seems to be something separate from them. *Sometimes I cannot tell whether I am still breathing or not.*"

When in a trance, then, the mystic shows all the usual signs of physical death: cessation of the pulse and respiration, coldness of the body and limbs, *rigor mortis,* suspension of the senses. And at the same time she experiences all the agonies of the rending —"the desire not to be parted," as she puts it, "which possesses the soul and body"—in other words, the horror of the 'passing'. But in the ardour of her faith the saint turns it to good account. While acknowledging "a great likeness" between "this elevation of the spirit" and death, she hastens to add: "We put aside the agonies of its dissolution, of which no great account is to be made; for they who love God in truth, and are utterly detached from the things of this life, must die with the greater sweetness."

What do these sufferings matter when they are rewarded by unimaginable enlightenment and joy? "The soul feels that it is in another region, entirely different from the one in which it usually dwells. It sees a light there incomparably more brilliant than that of this world, and in an instant it is instructed about innumerable amazing things, of which, however much it might strive, it could not imagine the thousandth part in several years." The most striking feature of these states is their intellectual element. The saint is "*instructed* about amazing things." And these notions are imparted to it by channels entirely different from the normal ones. The memory is discarded. "The will must be fully occupied in loving, but it understands not how it loves; the understanding, if it understands, does not understand how it understands." There is no doubt that the soul "feels," to use the saint's expression, for want of one more adequate. But what does it feel, and how? St. Teresa tells us that subsequently Christ revealed to her the state of the soul during these moments of ecstasy: "It undoes itself utterly, My daughter, in order that it may give itself more and more to Me: it is not itself that then lives; it is I. As it cannot comprehend what it understands, it understands by not understanding."

She admits in conclusion: "I do not understand it at all myself."

* * *

We shall not try to understand more than St. Teresa. We shall keep to the essence of the subject, the most solid element of her affirmations. And this, for our purpose, amounts to the fact that states of consciousness exist contemporaneously with all the signs of physical death—a fact which we knew already from the testimony of those who have escaped from death—and, what is of supreme importance, that, at a more advanced stage of actual death, a new form of consciousness—if one may continue to use the word—replaces the one with which we are acquainted.

But mystical states are quite exceptional. They provide us only with probabilities, not with the certainties that ordinary humanity requires. Let us descend from these heights and see how the 'passing' can be conceived and even sensed by those who are neither saints nor mystics.

Here is a letter from one of my confrères, who is a level-headed Catholic, though liable to sudden brief attacks of depression. His temperament is cheerful and his health is excellent, except for occasional heart trouble.

"As I am now over sixty years of age I may presume that I am approaching the end of my life. The thought does not frighten me in the least. In my normal state of mind and health death seems to me to be the simplest and easiest thing imaginable. I fancy that I have attained to such complete detachment that the final separation ought not to cause me any pain, so far as I can see. I even regard it as a happy event. Passion, which in any case is dead so far as I am concerned, has no new experience to offer me, and the world has nothing wonderful to show me. The unknown has practically ceased to interest me. The terrestrial lot of man leaves me unaffected. Human behaviour scandalizes me more and more. Accordingly I shall leave this world without regret, if not with joy.

"But when I go I want to be fully conscious, if that is possible. I don't want any drugs. I abhor injections of morphia or caffeine, anything that tries to cheat death and pain, anything that dulls our consciousness, that prolongs life artificially. So-called euthanasia is, in my opinion, a degradation, an interference with my liberty and will. In other words I don't want to die like a dog. If God grants me the use of my reason until the end I want to use it, so as to know and realize what is happening, even though it means realizing my suffering. I should be willing to suffer more if thereby I could detach myself even more completely. I trust in the goodness of God. I trust in Him absolutely. I am certain that His justice is totally different from human justice and that it has not the inhuman character of a law of Nature; otherwise His action would be no different from the mechanical action of the universe. For me, as even for the pagan philosophers, death is birth into eternity. That is why, when the time comes for me to go, I should like to be able to sing my *Magnificat*, my hymn of gratitude and humility, my acknowledgement of the fact that, insignificant as I am, I am permitted to indulge in such high hopes. . . ."

* * *

"I say all this to myself, I make these arrangements now, when I am enjoying more or less good health and my state of mind is normal. But things don't always go so easily as that. I have passed, and still pass, through periods of depression that leave disquieting memories behind them. During these periods I tell myself every evening that I am going to sleep with Death. And as I always mingle a little literature with my emotions I say to it: 'You are my pale betrothed, but that makes you no less charming!' I am in this state of apprehension because I expect to be awakened during the night by an anguish of pain that is probably the lot of all sufferers from heart disease.

"It is difficult, and probably impossible, to describe this anguish or any other emotional state to one who has not actually experienced it. It is mostly a physical sensation of oppression, or suffocation, painful enough but not excessively so. The effect of it on one's mind, however, is shattering. The physical part of the suffering is comparatively brief, and sometimes there is no pain at all, or if there is, it is scarcely appreciable. It is like dying by degrees, a listlessness of soul. One feels oneself detached and isolated from everything. The horizon is blotted out; there is nothing to be seen. One wants nothing, one hopes for nothing. The intellect and will are comatose. There is not the slightest desire to understand; there is no attempt to inquire into the causes of the malady. And curiously enough, although I firmly believe in God, I feel no need of Him, I have not even the strength to summon His assistance, to turn my thoughts to Him. It is a dismal stupor, though there is nothing terrible or tragic in it. It is a state of stagnancy, of infinite and hopeless dullness. . . .

"When I try to analyse my case I often think of the reply made by the dying Jules de Goncourt to his brother, who was watching the various stages of his agony and asked him anxiously: 'Where are you, friend?' 'In the great empty spaces,' came the answer. This is very much the impression I receive during the moments of which I have spoken just above. Then again I think of the remark made by Sainte-Beuve during the illness that was to bring about his death. 'Life, to me, is nothing now but a blank wall.' I, too, have the impression of a blank wall that shuts out the horizon for ever.

"Is it a foretaste of one's last moments, a prefiguration of the end? Up to now there has been only one occasion on which I thought I was going to die. It's a terrible sensation, quite different from the one already mentioned. The pain was not severe—in fact there may have been no pain at all. I woke up with a start and had the fearful sensation of being on the brink of death; I felt that though I might struggle with all my strength I should never survive another minute. I made a desperate effort of will, and the horror passed. I was left with the impression of having crossed a chasm. . . .

"I wonder if this is anything like the anguish of the 'passing'? Dare one think so? At such moments as I have spoken of, one thinks only of how to save one's life. It means a frantic effort on the part of the vital instinct. In the other state—that of the 'great empty spaces'—as I have already noted, one has not even the strength to pray. Is this meant to recall us to humility? Is God reminding us that without Him we can do nothing, not even call on Him for help?

"One comfort is that these states are not death itself, seeing that I am still alive. And in the second case I must have been very much alive, since it seems that it was only owing to my strength of will that I did not actually succumb. The fact is, we know nothing about the matter. We can only hope. I trust in the goodness of God; I trust that He will be with me at the 'passing', for I can do nothing if left to my own resources. I hope with all my heart that He will not fail me."

* * *

I have quoted this letter for the same reason that I have quoted extracts from the life of St. Teresa: because the things described therein have actually occurred and they have at least the merit of being genuine and sincere.

I need hardly say that the letter was not from my friend Perbal. He is much too busy a man to analyse himself in this way, and doubtless he thinks as I do, that we ought not to worry ourselves too much about the 'passing'. Personally, I shall not distress myself about the matter any further. I have examined it as best I could, and no doubt I shall revert to it at some future time. In any case, I am ready. I think I have the courage, but can one be certain of one's courage? If succour is necessary, I trust that it will be granted to me. And if there is another life—and I hope there will be—I am certain that it will be far superior to anything within my knowledge.

With God's help I shall cross the straits of death as I have crossed the straits of life.

CHAPTER VI

DEATH AS SEEN FROM A MONK'S CELL

THE last days I spent at the Escorial were marked by a great calm.

The calm was only within myself, for, outside, the weather was not at all conducive to collectedness and equanimity. Spring was near at hand, and squalls and showers followed each other in rapid succession, interspersed with intervals of faint illumination, during which, between its tears, the vast plain was bathed with short-lived rays of gold. The sky was restless, the air chilly and tumultuous, in a state of continual disturbance. My thoughts, too, had no consistency; they were as changeable as the weather. But in the midst of all this agitation a great peace reigned in the deepest depths of my soul, founded on the solid basis of my will. With regard to my fears of death I felt that my will was fixed, that my mind was made up, possibly for ever. This is the essential matter. And, though I did not realize it at the time, my inward disposition was strengthened, imperceptibly, by the symbolism of the Escorial, which, during my stay there, had gradually sunk into my mind and surrounded me with its soothing influences.

This colossal building, which has the appearance

of a granitic outgrowth of the mountain on which it rests, this work of perishable man, striving to make himself immortal till the end of time, is an act of faith that leaves no room for doubt. Here are no worries, no anguish of mind. The dogma that it represents seems as unshakable as its foundations; it has the solidity, the strict logic, of this geometrical construction in stone. The diagram of the human destiny is drawn there in a few bold, definite strokes as though engraved in bronze. This conception of destiny was that of the king who founded the monastery and the pantheon; no individual idea was allowed to mingle with it. If there was one, it was merged into Catholic thought, which is sole ruler here: we are in the world to work, to serve God, each of us in our different walks of life, so as to purify ourselves in preparation for the life of glory to which every single soul is called. Human grandeur serves merely as a pedestal for the majesty of God—*scabellum pedum tuorum*. Similarly, in this building of the Escorial, the precious marbles, polished as smooth as ebony, the glass, and the gilding of the *pudridero*, are only the pendant to the high altar, the dome, the airy spire, the gilded cross that is lost amid the clouds. . . .

To temper whatever rigour there might be in this conception, I had before my eyes a vast collection of paintings, sculptures, works in gold, exquisite material, all manner of rich and beautiful things. And all this in a natural setting of grandiose austerity, which, in its turn, is mitigated by the idyllic, agricultural aspect of the *huerta* round the

Escorial itself: great sheets of water, gushing fountains, flowers, vines, fruit-trees—a verdant oasis
nestling on the gloomy flank of the *sierra*, in view of
the bare and rugged plain. . . .

* * *

All these soothing influences, then, were having
their effect upon me when, the day before I left, I
thought I should like to assist at one of the numerous
Masses for the Dead that are celebrated every morning at various altars in the church. Catafalques,
decorated with black plumes and surmounted with
imperial, royal, or princely crowns, are always
there, ready to be moved by the sacristans from one
chapel to another, according to liturgical requirements. This stirring of macabre accoutrements,
these funereal rites, awakened within me gloomy
thoughts that had not troubled me for a long
time past. As a result, my mind was once again
plunged into a state of disorder such as had been
occasioned by my most wounding, most oppressive
griefs.

That evening, in my capacity of historian, I was
taken to the sinister chamber where the last of the
Spanish Habsburgs, the unhappy Charles II, known
to the Spaniards as *el hechizado*, 'the bewitched', was
exorcised as though he were actually in the possession of the Evil One. The monk who accompanied
me, one of the librarians of the Escorial and a
member of the Historical Academy at Madrid,
regaled me with every possible detail concerning

the terrifying ritual. The chamber, a veritable
garret, hidden away in a remote corner of the
monastery, a desolate symbol of the royal victim of
heredity, who had sunk to such a pitch as to believe
himself to be in the thrall of Satan—this and the
depressing, revolting thoughts evoked thereby, completed my mental agitation. We came back by way
of long, gloomy corridors that put me in mind of
the lugubrious, subterranean passages of the
Egyptian hypogea. I was ill at ease. Bygone terrors,
long since quelled, renewed their attack upon me
and weighed heavily on my spirits, while outside,
above our heads, great black clouds in the vernal
sky darkened the reddish surface of the Castilian
llanura. . . .

The Father took me to his cell, to show me its
magnificent view of the surrounding countryside.
The cell, which was on the highest storey of the
monastery, was a large room, with a lofty ceiling,
the beams of which were exposed to view, and walls
completely lined with books. The windows, which
seemed quite small from below, were actually very
large; they framed an immense horizon, with the
huerta of the Escorial in the foreground, and, stretching away infinitely far, the vast, undulating, rugged
plain, at the end of which a confused white blur was
visible from time to time.

"That's the Royal Palace at Madrid," the priest
explained, "and a little to the right of it is San
Francisco el Grande, just as they appear in Goya's
famous picture. . . . Do you remember it? . . . It's
in the Prado. . . . The Pradera de San Isidro. . . ."

But I was incapable of appreciating anything. I scarcely listened to him as he extolled the beauties of the view, the delightful situation of his cell, the consolations of monastic life, a wholly spiritual life lived in the midst of Nature. Finally I revealed to him the sad state in which my mind had been since morning. . . . Making no reply, he went to his table and picked up an old volume with beautiful clasps and binding. It was a translation in Castilian of the opuscule by Louis de Blois, Abbot of Lessies, in Belgium—the *Consolatio Pusillanimium*.

"This was the actual copy," said the monk, "used by our founder, Philip II. It was his bedside book for many years, and during his last illness he either read it himself or had it read to him by one of his chaplains, when his fingers were so eaten away by ulcers that it was impossible for him to hold it. . . . That took place quite near to where we are. You can easily picture the scene to yourself. You have seen the cell where he died—just like any one of ours—the narrow alcove where he had his bed, and the dormer in the bare wall which gave him a view of the high altar. Lying in agony on his pallet, he could see the priest celebrating Mass, he could see him raising the Host, the sign of ransom. . . . And to calm his fears the chaplain read him this. . . ."

The priest turned over the pages of the old book that had been worn yellow by the royal hand, and he in his turn read me the following lines, on hearing which I felt that there was nothing more to say.

They are the words of Christ speaking to the dying:

I AM THY SALVATION: BE NOT AFRAID.

LET NOT THY INIQUITIES AFFRIGHT THEE:

I AM THE ADVOCATE FOR THE GUILTY.

FEAR NOT THE DARKNESS:

I AM THE LIGHT.

FEAR NOT DEATH:

I AM THE LIFE.

FEAR NOT DAMNATION:

I AM THE REDEEMER.